OPERAS ON AMERICAN SUBJECTS

H. EARLE JOHNSON

Operas on American Subjects

COLEMAN-ROSS COMPANY, INC.
1964 NEW YORK

Coleman-Ross Company, Inc., New York 36, N. Y.

Manufactured in the United States of America

Library of Congress Catalog Card Number: 64-17352

To

FLORENCE CHANDLER

CONTENTS

OVERTURE

"If there's no meaning in it," said the King, "that saves a world of trouble, you know, as we needn't try to find any. And yet I don't know," he went on, spreading out the verses on his knee, and looking at them with one eye, "I seem to see some meaning in them, after all."

ALICE IN WONDERLAND

OVERTURE

Viewing the panoramic canvases of Benjamin West, John Trumbull, the Peales, Washington Allston, or other painters of an older tradition and heroic day, we may readily visualize them as impressive ensembles in the style of grand opera. We stand enraptured before these craftsmanlike realizations of significant moments in human history, grateful to the artist whose patriotic vision has outlined eloquent lessons for our time. If, at these moments, we allow ourselves to be caught up in the full sweep of American political and social drama, we may fancy that great music is surging through the galleries to revivify and intensify their meaning.[1]

The martial air and thunder of cannon are inseparable in the history of warfare, since music has traditionally accompanied marching troops as a moral incitation to victory. Only in modern times have the rumble of tanks and the uproar of aircraft made futile the more grateful strains of melody. If these earlier customs seem at this remove to give an oddly sporting cast to sober pursuits, we can only accept them as being of custom long venerated, and note that causes for which men fought then were every whit as momentous as those of the present.

---

[1] A few of the best-known subjects are: West: *William Penn's Treaty with the Indians* (c. 1771), *The Death of Wolfe* (1772); Trumbull: *Death of General Warren at the Battle of Bunker Hill* (1775), *Capture of the Hessians at Trenton* (1781), *Surrender of Lord Cornwallis at Yorktown* (1799), *Surrender of General Burgoyne at Saratoga* (1816), *Declaration of Independence* (1786-97), *General Washington Resigning His Commission* (1817-1822); C. S. Peale: *Washington at Valley Forge;* Krimmel: *Fourth of July in Central Square* (c. 1815); and Archibald Willard's *Spirit of '76,* in Abbott Hall, Marblehead, Massachusetts (1876).

As we stand in spacious galleries of museums and historical societies, before civic monuments in and out of doors, our subjective visualizations of great music are reasonable and appropriate. The grave instance at the conference table, the solemn hush in moments of surrender, the utterance of immortal words before a moved throng, all become fraught with deeper meaning to the individual whose musical sensibilities enable him to clothe all with an aura of highlighting art.

The time will come — must yet come, for only in the slightest measure is it now with us — when the colorful, stirring events brilliantly commemorated by American painters, sculptors, novelists, and poets will find worthy parallels in the art of music. The resulting scores will be as exalting in their sphere as are the noble panegyrics spoken from the platform or brave deeds on the battlefields in symbolizing the potent drama of freedom, and they will sound with the same clear urgency.

It is unthinkable that the subject-matter of grand opera must of necessity be European in order to gain artistic merit or popular acclaim, even though the current repertory implies as much. The story of America from 1492 to the present, from Baffin Bay to the South Pole, offers precisely those qualities inherent in good librettos. Scenes and events in our history are of such sweep and grandeur that we may expect that music highlighting their drama will possess a quality superior to the music of 19th-century *verismo* or 20th-century mechanistic realism, which magnifies improbable, sordid, or trivial situations. These new American musical documents may be classic, romantic, or modern according to preference. They may be of "tragedy, comedy, history, pastoral, pastoral-comical, historical-pastoral, tragical-historical, tragical-comical-historical-pastoral, scene individual, or poem unlimited," and prove this catalogue incomplete.

When the layman approaches the subject of opera in American life he is wont to try his energies in argument over opera in the vernacular. But we will not often disagree on the proposition that the vast panorama of our history, ranging from discovery, exploration, and unfolding settlement, to present-day social conflict in all its ramifications, provides an abundance of possibilities brilliantly appropriate to the operatic medium. There is not a quality known to human experience, credible or incredible, lacking in the eventful, tortuous, heroic, or inglorious episodes which combine to make the nations of the Western Hemisphere what they are today. Close association with our own substantial traditions, now firm as foundation yet fresh with novelty, insures a verisimilitude and trenchancy rarely possible to classic mythologies, the French Revolution, the petty court intrigues of the 18th and 19th centuries, or domestic life on the impoverished estates of Europe's landed gentry.

All but the uninformed may be under the impression that, operatically speaking, composers have not yet discovered America or given her people a considerate thought. Such is not the case. The American subject, it may be said, has preyed on the minds of many whose earnestness has not been matched by a commensurate talent. The world of art is permitted liberties and luxuries which the world of business cannot afford, among them simplification and stereotype. Hence some very odd manifestations have come and gone in the name of American opera. One might hope that, after nearly 350 years of settlement and 200 years of independence, more frequent signs of maturity might be brought to light.

To the English composer of ballad operas (or comedy-operas, as some scholars prefer to call them), America was populated by Indians and nought else. He had seen Indians, inasmuch as such novelties were exhibited abroad before delighted audiences. In 1710 Col. Schuyler took four Indian "Chiefs" to London, where they attracted curiosity throughout the Kingdom. Addison wrote a *Spectator* paper on them,[2] and Swift mentions them in his letters to Stella; they called on the Queen and recited a poem in her honor. Other Red Men were seen on the Strand throughout the 18th century, while real and imaginary tales were printed in magazines and books of the day. By comparison, the British-American settler of the New World seemed tame and colorless to the dramatist. He did not often figure on the operatic stage until the late 19th century, when a group of composers turned to the Pilgrims, Merry Mount, and *The Scarlet Letter.*

Ballad operas are invariably indefinite as to location. Constant adaptation allowed for sea-changes with far greater ease than the rather unhappy transmigration of Verdi's *The Masked Ball* from Naples to Boston. Hence definite identification of the setting in certain ballad operas is difficult, particularly if there are no Indians to help us. *The Quaker* by Charles Dibdin, as Sonneck notes, was probably given a native color wherever it was sung. *True Blue,* adapted from Carey's *Nancy,* was changed to include a scene at the Battery in New York, while Shield's *The Poor Soldier,* originally entitled *The Shamrock,* appeared to American audiences as the adventures of a gallant continental. Even as late as Michael Balfe (see *The Maid of Artois*), published scores often remained tantalizingly incomplete in citing their localities.

---

[2] *The Spectator,* No. 50: "Indian Kings in England: Extracts from Their Journal." Also, No. 56, "The Tale of Marraton." Neither of these articles gives any description of the Indians.

A set of portraits of these "Chiefs" — they were not chiefs at all — is extant. Richmond P. Bond, in his *Queen Anne's American Kings* (Oxford, 1952) treats them exhaustively.

Sonneck also points out that American managers frequently gave new titles to their importations.

We may note the potency of some early librettos. *Tammany* may have been wretched stuff in the eyes of critics, but it was sufficiently point-blank to curl the hair of certain New York politicians. *Disappointment; or, The Force of Credulity* was not produced at all because it ridiculed certain easily identifiable Philadelphia citizens. We may trace a line, somewhat interrupted during the 19th century, from these works to those of Krenek, Hindemith, Blitzstein, and Antheil, and note that before opera was attenuated by excessive romanticism, the virile truths of salient commentary were developed into social and political satire which is nowadays treated only with success in a few musical comedies and occasional motion pictures. *Susannah* is a lineal descendant of *The Scarlet Letter,* for Arthur Dimmesdale and Olin Blitch have the same basic characteristics, although our sympathies may be with the former. The clergyman in *Merry Mount* is of the same category.

* * * * *

There are two Americas. That belonging to Spain was the more popular in the 19th century, and continental composers turned to it for ideas. Columbus, Montezuma, Cortez, and Pizarro were given their share of regard. Columbus, leading all others, is still favored, as the names of Juárez and Maximilian extend the Spanish-American subject almost to our own day. According to Julius Mattfeld, whose coverage of New York is authoritative and complete, no grand opera on Columbus, Ponce de León, Pizarro, or Montezuma has been performed in that city, and his statement probably holds for all North America above Mexico. Spontini's *Fernand Cortez* was done briefly at the Metropolitan. For that matter, Merry Mounts, Hiawathas, and Sleepy Hollows are not common to South America, but the twain might be persuaded to meet were the quality of works sufficiently high to warrant a universal audience.

The earliest scores on these discoverers and navigators offer an occasional conflict with the savage Indian, but their writers were realistic enough to know that the Red Man does not sing in *bel canto;* hence a few lines of recitative and the ballet suffice for him. We may surmise that the Indian was better served in earlier ballad works where he remains either comic or exotic. Composers both of English ballad operas and of Italian *opera seria,* however, were practised craftsmen, and their total efforts were successful even if their Indians were not. The ballets, a medley of Russian terpsichore, Negro shuffle, and artless prancing — certainly not Indian — were given costumes that were recognizable if not authentic.

Rural America, or the Yankee tradition, might have come into its own much earlier had it not been for the introduction of Italian opera. Hawkins' *The Saw Mill; or, A Yankee Trick,* and Davies' *The Forest Rose; or, The American Farmers* derived from the ballad opera. Davies' work was produced in New York on October 7, 1825. These two were American inside and out, but their influence was halted by the arrival of the Garcia troupe, when on November 29, 1825, Italian opera was introduced to the Northern Hemisphere. (It is worth noting that James Fenimore Cooper was in the John St. Theater on this historic first night.)

* * * * *

When conscience pricked men and women of the late 19th and the first quarter of the 20th century into a combined literary and musical crusade involving grand opera, the crises multiplied. Adaptation of a fine literary work does not insure an acceptable libretto. With *The Last of the Mohicans, The Scarlet Letter, Rip van Winkle,* and the poems of Longfellow to draw upon, the pace advanced markedly and verisimilitude tottered in its stride. Wagner was being grandiloquently literary in Germany, the books of French grand opera were from the accomplished Scribe, and Verdi drew heavily on Victor Hugo and Shakespeare. After all, Mozart had his da Ponte to adapt Beaumarchais, and Gluck his Calzabigi. Why should not accredited American works serve composers well? Indeed, they should, and we may examine librettos drawn from Cooper, Hawthorne, Irving, and Longfellow with varying interest. Examining the scores, however, we see that literary distinction was ours at least half a century before we acquired a musical voice of our own. Therein lay the problem. The absolute demands of opera, exemplified time and time again in the current repertory, are primarily musical, and only remotely literary. The constant demand for a closer union, a fairer balance between the two, remains largely unfulfilled.

We may note that in instances of critical judgment given in these pages, the libretto is often deemed inferior to the music. Sobolewski, Herbert, Hadley, Hanson, and Copland have not been companioned by writers of equal ability. *The Emperor Jones* is an exception wherein the story is praised at the expense of the music. In view of the veriest nonsense contained in works currently popular, one might be inclined to dismiss the libretto as not very important after all. But as the structure on which the artistic unity of the whole must be built, it is apparent that a good libretto is at least a great help.

Briefly analyzing the nature of the literary subjects thus far selected for opera on this broad canvas, we may consider whether or not there are definite stylistic trends. One hesitates to pronounce a verdict of failure or success without fuller examination of scores or, for that matter, without hearing them in performance. Press notices are useful but not conclusive, for the history of criticism is a history of contemporary thought and not a harbinger of changing taste. Success may still lie hidden from present sight in some of these temporary victories, or even in summarily rejected failures.

Over a period of two centuries, and on two rapidly expanding continents, there will be many trends to observe. Differing approaches to form, idiom, subject-matter, and general treatment will carry well-wrought works in so many directions that only the central fact of opera as a stage work to be sung remains to bind them together. The lists following this essay speak more conclusively than any argument.

Music of almost two centuries is here represented, omitting for the most part the barren second quarter of the 19th century. Nearly all the nations of Europe have tried their skills, and composers in every section of America have imitated these European styles, without which we would not have the form of opera. We cannot put the talents of the weakest amateurs with those of resourceful professionals, shake them together, and expect the ingredients to blend into a unified strain. Works composed since the second quarter of the present century — a period which some consider strongly formative of a native school of composition — are already labelled after seven years as "aging rapidly" (cf. Thomson's *The Mother of Us All*). The fact remains clear that the style is the man.

* * * * *

The Indian, as an operatic figure, has probably gone the way of his cigar-store counterpart, and is not likely to be in fashion again. The devotion to his cause by Cadman, Skilton, Lieurance, Gilbert, and others will not be greatly respected in the future. But the period of Spanish exploration, with Columbus as a rallying figure, appears more valid, although it does not present an easy approach. Strangely, it has been entirely rejected thus far by North American composers. The actual personalities of these discoverers and navigators are historically vague; hence their portrayal in terms of romantic or heroic stock images is more easily accepted than will be the case with 19th-century leaders whose biographies are minutely documented, and whose aspect and manner are clear in the public mind.

The subjects given here do not provide an exhaustive list. North American composers have favored the literary rather than the historical theme, while the reverse is true in South America. It is amazing that, out of nearly three hundred entries, none of the great episodes of our national past are approached. Neither Bradford, Franklin, Jefferson, Lee, Sherman, nor Dewey — to name only a few dramatic figures — has received a real hearing. Patrick Henry and Alexander Hamilton, both of whom were capable of a fine fury, are not to be found. Surely there's a fine baritone among the lot! We may note, parenthetically, that the Roosevelts and Truman have turned up in musical comedies of superior quality. Even the Indian might have another day if Daniel Boone, Lewis and Clark, or General Custer were given voices. The most obvious gesture in the direction of politics is Antheil's *Transatlantic,* written in the disenchanted twenties and produced in Germany, where its plot must have added to the mounting disrespect for democratic dogma.

Memorable episodes in national history often provide the subject for pageants; but pageants are ponderously static affairs in comparison to operatic production. The landing of the Pilgrims, the signing of the Declaration of Independence, the winter at Valley Forge, William Penn and the Indians — these come to mind as possibilities.

No operatic composer has approached the figure of Lincoln. Daniel Webster, George Washington, "Stonewall" Jackson, Ulysses S. Grant, and Martin van Buren are present in these scores, but not (with the exception of Daniel Webster) in leading roles. Events of the Revolution, the Boston Tea Party, Bunker Hill, Paul Revere and his midnight ride, episodes in the history of the *Constitution,* strong men of their times: Ethan Allen, Nathan Hale, Major André, Lafayette, Benedict Arnold, Aaron Burr, Lord Cornwallis — these also cry out for a composer to heighten their drama. The War of 1812 and the Civil War awaken slight response in the composer of works for the lyric stage. The pen waits for breath to set down the names of men and events in war and in peace to which music can give a loftier emphasis.

Rampant enthusiasm for the American Indian during the first quarter of the present century may be surprising to us at this remove. As late as 1920 the opinion was firmly held by men and women of undoubted sincerity that the only true American music *was* Indian, that the white man had none of his own, and that the future of American art must inevitably derive from that premise. There was also a similarly mistaken notion regarding the Negro. In the train of Skilton, Gilbert, and Cadman were less competent musicians, including many eager women, who wrote, produced, and usually paid the production costs of their own grand operas. Lois Albright, Eleanor Everest Freer, and Mary Carr Moore were composers of five works utilizing their own librettos, while Cadman and Skilton wrote six works to librettos by three lady writers. Other people who had never written a song or harmonized a chorale plunged into the composition of grand operas on Wakuta, Winona, Natoma, Mohega, Wa-Kin-Yon, or the White Buffalo Maiden, each one a daughter of the forest "done wrong" by the white man. In retrospect these appear even less successful, surely less amusing, than Hewitt's Tammany or Storace's Cherokee. The Indian was not only explored, he was exploited, and the results, surveyed from the present, are not impressive.[3]

The intrepidity of these men and women is wonderful to behold, and the goodwill of their friends and supporters touching beyond measure. Few desisted after one try, although their remaining operas often strayed from the American course. Many of these North American composers — so unlike the general — were persons of unlimited leisure and private wealth, and there were patrons generous to a fault. It is misleading, therefore, to report the number of performances as indexes of quality. (We may cite, parenthetically, Legrand Howland's *Sarrona; or, The Indian Slave* [1903], on an Asiatic subject, which was sung two hundred times in the opera houses of Europe, but had only a single matinee performance at the New Amsterdam Theater in New York, and was given once in German at the Saake German Theater in Philadelphia.) A number of composers coyly mention that their scores were favorably considered by the Opéra-Comique or by the Metropolitan, but something happened to prevent production. A score mislaid by Heinrich Conried, manager of the Metropolitan, brought about a lawsuit for its recovery; and we may praise the modesty, at least, of another who "was too much of a gentleman at heart to push himself forward"; therefore his music is not well known.

The composer whose Anglo-American heritage was uppermost in thought seconded the statement of Walt Whitman, himself an unabashed enthusiast of opera. In *Gathering of the Forces,* Part II, Whitman wrote:

> We do wish the good ladies and gentlemen of America would be true to themselves and to legitimate refinement. With all honor and glory to the land of the olive tree and the vine, fair-skied Italy — with no turning up of noses at Germany, France, or England — we humbly demand whether we have not run after their beauties long enough. For nearly every nation has its peculiarities with its idioms which make its best intellectual efforts dearest to itself alone, so that hardly anything which comes to us in the music and songs of the Old World, is strictly good and fitting to our nation.

---

[3] A few, at the other extreme, were successful authors of harmony texts or books on how to write music:

Chadwick, George Whitefield: *Harmony, A Course of Study* (Boston: B. F. Wood, 31st ed. 1897)

Pasmore, Henry B. and Toreck, Paul, translators: Jadassohn: *Manual of Harmony.* This work had at least nine editions.

Patterson, Franklin B.: *How to Write a Good Tune* (New York: G. Schirmer, 1925)

Southard, Lucien: *Course of Harmony* (Boston: Reed, 1855); *Elements of Thoroughbass and Harmony* (Boston: Oliver Ditson, 1867)

Strube, Gustav: *The Theory and Use of Chords: a Textbook of Harmony* (Boston: Oliver Ditson, 1928)

That Whitman's voice was raised in anticipation rather than upon fulfillment is evident from the record.

* * * * *

Musical styles began with English ballad opera by Reinagle, Pelissier, and Raynor Taylor. The adumbrations of continental grand opera commenced a century later with Bristow, Fry, and Maretzek whose works were respectful imitations of Bellini, Donizetti, and Rossini. Musical sophisticates later demanded imitation of Wagner, as Hadley, Maryon, and Damrosch adopted systems of leitmotifs whereby each character or idea was labelled like so many jars of homemade jelly on the pantry shelf. Those who leaned toward Puccini, whose effect springs from inner passion rather than outwardly contrived system, utterly failed. Works composed between the two World Wars, by Antheil, Thomson, and Blitzstein, often written abroad, reveal their cerebral debt to Hindemith, Krenek, Stravinsky, or other continental influences. Meanwhile, in America's "out West," the type of musical thinking current was unable to profit by anyone at all, let alone to stand securely on its own feet.

The student of European music will note with pleasure that celebrated composers drew on American themes, though with no intent to compliment us other than by believing that the stories were dramatically and musically effective. To find Auber, Donizetti, Dussek, Grétry, Halévy, Hummel, Lortzing, Méhul, Paisiello, Planquette, Piccini, and Rossini in this company is pleasing nonetheless. Of all nations, Peru had the most romantic appeal, because of Kotzebue's *Die Spanier in Peru.*

Operas by the Romantic composers involved legendary characters frequently displaying supernatural powers, and the *buffa* operas were caricatures of persons living, or of those who could easily qualify as recognizable types. The United States today can parallel these types in folklore, yet they are ignored except for *Boney Quillen, The Devil and Daniel Webster, The Mighty Casey* and, of course, the eternal *Rip van Winkle.* The comic genius may be more difficult to portray than the tragic, but the fact remains that most of the operas listed here are serious dramas from whatever angle one surveys them.

But where are Davy Crockett, Mike Fink, Buffalo Bill, Roy Bean, Paul Bunyan, John Henry, Johnny Appleseed, all the Texans, and members of the Liars Club? There are comic figures in American literature and folklore to parallel all of Europe's vampires and sorcerers, and even Mephistopheles himself; we have counterparts of Figaro, Papageno, Leporello, Beckmesser, Don Pasquale, and Baron Ochs, to mention only a few.

We need not be astonished that European composers treating America from the point of view of its discovery by Italian and Spanish heroes favored the colorful native character of the Indian, or drew upon the fantastic qualities of Rip van Winkle and Robinson Crusoe. The universal nature of the situations and emotions involved was more important in their works than historical accuracy. But it is unexplainable that composers of the United States have avoided the larger issues of the Revolution, have failed to go forward with the expanding West, to mark the cowboy, the frontiersman, the "Forty-Niners," or take up Lincoln as a symbol of nobility, to fight musically at Gettysburg, relight the Chicago and San Francisco fires, revel in instances and objects of historical and fictional color, sail with clipper ship fact and romance, or indulge in the slave trade. Only the wry humorist will seriously imply that, in view of the general impermanence of the scores listed in these pages, we have been so far fortunate.

Sixty years ago Teddy Roosevelt was reprimanding American painters for being less interested in Fulton Market than in the picturesque market places of Europe. "The Bowery is one of the great highways of humanity, a highway of seething life, of varied interest, of fun, of work, of sordid and terrible tragedy; and it is haunted by demons as evil as any that stalk through the pages of Dante's *The Inferno,*" he declared. Painters and literary men took up the challenge — Stephen Crane, Frank Norris, Dreiser, John Sloan, George Luks, Bellows, and Glackens. Roosevelt might have included American composers who were being grim with Puritan maids or prettifying the Indian.

A generation later E. Bruce Knowlton tried to encompass the lumber and mining backgrounds of the Northwest; Converse composed a most interesting work (unproduced) on immigrants entering at Ellis Island; Damrosch in two works touched on Aaron Burr and Stephen Decatur, the United States Navy and the Senate Chamber in Washington; and Kurt Weill gave us *Street Scene* in teeming New York. But these dynamic subjects are not numerous in view of the whole.

The conclusion is inevitable that the much-abused Hollywood is more forward-looking in its exploration of this historic past. We frequently cite the cost of producing an opera, an argument impossible to refute, but it is only fractional of the cost of an Hollywood epic. The answer lies not in the cost but in the reward. Is the cinema public more receptive to the sweep of our history than the supposedly sophisticated musical audience? Must the five-million-dollar film make another five million in profits while the hundred-thousand-dollar operatic production expires after four ill-attended performances? Assuredly the film of *Northwest Passage,* or a Class B remake of *The Last of the Mohicans* is not more worthy than Hanson's *Merry Mount* as a work of either art or entertainment. There is something to be said for the open-mindedness of a less critical public which cooperates by gladly taking a first look, leaving final judgment to the professionals and to posterity.

It is heartening to note the acclaim greeting many operas on American subjects by the general public. Large and fashionable audiences loyally attended the first performances of works by George F. Bristow, Walter Damrosch, Henry Hadley, and Victor Herbert in loyal support of an idea and of a friend. This abundance of goodwill added that tentative involvement with success which only an audience can contribute. Were good wishes the balancing criteria, we would now enjoy a modest number of successful operas in this genre. The customarily dim aftermath supplied by the critics seems inappropriate to the festive nature of the openings; yet time, in its inexorable course, upholds the severer verdict. Critics are sometimes mistaken; a glance at statements made about *Madama Butterfly* and *The Girl of the Golden West* proves their fallibility.

We are here treating of musical composition which is often — not always — unimaginative and imitative, while quoting critics of an era already distinctive in American music and letters. The names of John Sullivan Dwight, Richard Storrs Willis, and George Putnam Upton, foundation stones in American music criticism in Boston, New York, and Chicago, were followed by William F. Apthorp, James Gibbons Huneker, H. E. Krehbiel, Philip Hale, Pitts Sanborn, H. T. Parker, Richard Aldrich, W. J. Henderson, and Lawrence Gilman, the brightest stars in a dazzling firmament. They may be equalled but not surpassed in our time. These were men of learning, of background in music and letters, of foreign travel; they were literary practitioners whose editors offered unlimited space for analysis and reflection. There is great need for an anthology of American musical criticism of this Golden Age.

Audiences were as eager for success as were those involved in productions. Although an American subject was incidental to this enthusiasm, there were many who looked forward to the day when our land would be freed from its entire dependence on European culture, as it was rapidly becoming independent in economics and had already achieved distinction in democratic government. The ringing challenge of Emerson still echoed in the minds of many:

> We have listened too long to the courtly muses of Europe. The spirit of the American freeman is already suspected to be timid, imitative, tame.[4]

Emerson's words were spoken only eighteen years before Bristow, at the age of thirty, produced his *Rip van Winkle.* As an angry young man of his time, Bristow received them as words of passionate protest.

---

[4] *The American Scholar,* an oration delivered at Cambridge, August 31, 1837.

> What is the remedy? [Emerson goes on.] If the single man plant himself indomitably on his instincts, and there abide, the huge world will come around to him. Patience — patience; with the shades of all the good and great for company; and for solace, the perspective of your own infinite life; and for work, the communication of principles, the making of those instincts prevalent, the conversion of the world.

Those who fought for Bristow's work were fighting for more than an opera. Their polemics were, in the long run, of far greater value than his *Rip van Winkle.*

Bristow's conviction, however, was that an American should write a good European opera. Walt Whitman, in an odd passage, made notes of a more native concept which most composers of his time would have rejected as false.

> American opera — put three banjos (or more?) in the orchestra — and let them accompany (at times exclusively) the songs of the baritone or tenor — let a considerable part of the performance be instrumental — by the orchestra only — let a few words go a great ways — the plot not complicated but simple — Always one leading idea — as Friendship, Gratitude, Courage, Love — and always a distinct meaning — the story and libretto as now generally of no account — In the American opera the story and libretto must be in the body of the performance.[5]

* * * * *

A healthy feature of our operatic experience is the extent of participation in sponsoring works by American composers. The Seguin Company brought out Fry's *Leonora* in 1845; in 1855, Ole Bull offered $1,000 "for the best original grand opera, by an American composer, upon a strictly *American subject*," but his enterprise collapsed within a few weeks and there is no reason to suppose that the results of his contest could have prolonged it. Theodore Thomas' American Opera Company (sponsored by Mrs. Jeannette Thurber during the seasons 1885-1887) sang works by American composers, and the Emma Juch Opera Company (1889-1891) did likewise. The Metropolitan's record is not long, but its examples are representative. The Chicago Opera Company was even more receptive to this idea. The American Grand Opera Company (under slightly differing titles), centering its activities in Portland, Oregon, brought forth several works in the 1920's, all markedly conservative in taste. In the same years the subsidized opera houses of Germany were trying experiments of the most extreme sorts, on occasion

[5] Robert D. Faner, *Walt Whitman and Opera* (Phila.: University of Pennsylvania Press, 1951).

involving American scores. In both situations private financing provided a life-giving benefaction; such are the annals of the operatic world.

The National Federation of Music Clubs (founded in 1898) is ever earnest in its cause, for ten of the operas listed here are by women who emulated Wagner by serving as their own librettists. (Their emulation ceased at that point.) As noted, women were also librettists for a number of works composed by men. Overwhelmingly, these ladies were enamored of the Indian, and the Sioux lead all the rest as an operatic tribe.

What areas of the United States have been most active in furthering the native as an operatic hero? All things considered, the Pacific Northwest. The part of the country that was least often visited by Italian opera evolved its own. Portland, Oregon, had the American Grand Opera Company; other works were produced in Seattle and in Provo, Utah. A number of Midwestern cities sponsored new works. (It is in order for Easterners to recall that New Orleans, Mexico City, Rio de Janeiro, and Lima have a notable operatic past, and that Los Angeles heard the first performance in America of *La Bohème.* Grand opera does not unfailingly enter at the port of New York.) We may be surprised to find operatic ambitions in persons born in Vermont which, with Utah, enjoys fewer operatic performances per annum than other states. We may mistrust the merit of works by composers impelled to establish their own companies, as Freeman, Knowlton, or Mrs. Gerrish Jones, but a few existing organizations here and abroad were *persuaded,* for a consideration, to mount works, and we never shall know whether Arthur Nevin paid for a hearing of his *Poia* in Berlin.

A happy fact may be noted in the role played by colleges and universities whose facilities continue to encourage works that might otherwise never come into being or, having come into being, might have had less fortunate sponsorship. Educational institutions are now judiciously playing the part formerly sustained by the whims of well-to-do patrons. These music schools and colleges have also led to a type of intimate opera which is of great value in itself as well as being a proving ground for the developing composer. Works by the following have been first presented in university theaters:

Ernst Bacon
Jack Beeson
Robert Russell Bennett
Philip Bezanson
Alberto Bimboni
Carlisle Floyd
Lukas Foss
Herbert Haufrecht
Walter Kaufmann
Arthur Kreutz
Normand Lockwood
Douglas Moore
Jan Meyerowitz
William Schuman
Virgil Thomson
Felix Vinatieri
Max Wald
Kurt Weill

This type of sponsorship is not characteristic of any other country.

America has been in the forefront in producing singers of high calibre. In the days of Bristow's struggle, many Americans went abroad for study. Some sang in European opera houses, several became famous as instrumentalists, and a scholar or two was even then doing important research. Composers were having their orchestral and chamber works played. We know that nearly a hundred of these young Americans were in Germany, Italy, and Spain before 1860 — one American singer just missed becoming Queen of Spain — and that they paralleled the painters, sculptors, and literary figures whose careers are better known.

Were we alert to these things, the manager of the Metropolitan Opera would not have gained wide publicity in 1954 by saying that "there just weren't any American interpreters of opera" before 1936. Yet this is a common opinion. What are the facts? Briefly, that the second performance at the Metropolitan (1883) included an American, that sixteen Americans were there before 1900, and 178 between the opening and 1936. The Chicago Opera listed 248 American singers on its roster between 1910 and 1936. Not all were stars, but they included Hauk, Albani, Eames, Fremstad, Juch, Nevada, Nordica, and Bispham — all before 1900.

In consort with their interest in American artists, European audiences have always been openly intrigued by the American subject. This contrasts with American audiences, which were willing to look up to the native composer while looking down on the native theme. Many of the composers listed here wrote operas on other than American subjects, and often with greater success, a fact signifying only that we need not accept the work given here as typical of the best. Only by the merit of his music does a composer prove what is that best of all subjects. Who shall say, for instance, that *Wakuta* is inferior to, or more outdated, than *Transatlantic?*

Mark Twain showed his preference. "I think in the Jubilees and their songs America has produced the perfect flower of the ages; and I wish it were a foreign product, so that she could worship it and lavish money on it and go properly crazy over it." His opinion, tongue-in-cheek though it may be, serves as a reaction to the extreme artiness of certain American segments, as well as a disparagement of foreign idols. What would Twain have thought of *Porgy and Bess,* the works of Douglas Moore, or half a dozen other successful native productions?

* * * * *

Rigid definition of the word "opera" is impossible. These works are taken at face value, and I would not be their judge, not even if *every* score had been examined. Nearly all published sources have been carefully looked at, plus a few available manuscripts, or copies, inasmuch as the dust has settled on many an old score in libraries. And I have taken the word of composers who have been kind enough to write me. However, a few items may be brought into question. Ballad works of the past are here, inasmuch as they served until 1825 when opera was made known in America. The modern musical comedy is excluded.[6] For our own day I have tried to make a distinction between grand and light opera (operetta), but plainly the light ones were often heavy, and the heavy ones far too light. Yes, we have no Bellinis today.

All, nonetheless, aspired to be operas. All aspired to be successes as well, and that which constitutes success may be a matter of individual interpretation, as well as a matter of popular support. Others whose moribund fate I have not as yet unearthed, or whose complete documentation seems unobtainable, are given by title, together with an admission of defeat. This must be taken as a basic list to which others will be added through the kindness of fellow scholars or of composers themselves.

I have resisted the appeal of J. C. F. Bach's Cantata, *Die Amerikanerin,* the overtures of Bristow, Wagner, and Lauro on the subject of Columbus, and Lauro's orchestral poem *America,* as irrelevant to this study. It was easier to forego two Boy Scout operas and one for the Camp Fire Girls.

At times there is a subtle distinction to be made between a historical subject, a national type, or a literary adaptation, such as Blitzstein's *Regina* which renders them of doubtful inclusion. Operas on Robinson Crusoe are admitted because his island bower was at the mouth of the Orinoco River. (Robinson, by the way, did not lack female companionship. The day of *Billy Budd* and the all-male cast was far distant.) There is no absolute distinction made between works done at the Metropolitan, for instance, and those done on Broadway. How merciful that *Porgy and Bess* was spared production by an opera company!

A continuing perplexity is the lack of basic information about many American composers. Writing for opera is not always one aspect of a wider purpose encompassing symphonies and chamber music. Successful composers of operas — Meyerbeer, Wagner, Verdi, or Puccini — for the most part confined their writing to works for the stage. But that such men as E. Earle Blakeslee, Max Faetkenhauer, Henry Lincoln Case, A. J. Davis, William F. Hanson, F. S. Hyde, and many others are unknown, often to the libraries or historical societies of their own communities, is more surprising than the lack of information on certain

[6] A scholarly survey of this typically American form of entertainment would be of great service in giving substance to several general works now current. Cecil Smith's *Musical Comedy in America* (New York: Theatre Arts, 1950), and David Ewen's *Complete Book of the American Musical Theater,* (New York: Holt, 1958) are starts in the right direction.

South American and Italian composers. Efforts to give credit where credit is due is defeated by the paucity of biographical dictionaries treating of musical life in the New World.

In particular Edward Maryon may be cited. Born in England, trained in Germany, and long resident in the United States, Maryon was a highly skilled technician. His orchestral scores are complex, precise, and somewhat revolutionary; they prove a technical mastery suggestive of Richard Wagner. But most of all they show a rare spirit of dedication by one who heard but little of his music performed. To those readers who suspect other works in this list to be little more than a crude stringing together of tunes, the instance of Edward Maryon will give pause insofar as their competency is concerned. Carl Venth is another composer of proven technical ability.

That which remains witnesses a substantial body of interest in the operatic form, shows a persistence often worthy of better fortune, and proves that America as a subject, if not yet firmly in hand, has never been out of mind.

It would seem that these works are broad enough in coverage to stake out the field for all time, inasmuch as they range from Gerard Tonning's *Leif Erikson* and de Rogatis' *Huemac* (on a subject dating from 600 A.D.) to jazz operas, works with scenes in Childs Restaurant in Times Square, and Jan Meyerowitz' opera on race relations in the South. The earliest European ballad opera with an American subject was apparently Anfossi's *L'Americana in Olanda* (Venice, 1778), but the Indians are still with us. Miss Lois Albright's *Hopitu* was sung (in concert) at Carnegie Hall during February, 1955, "ancient Hopi legends," "primitive chants" and all. The Indian warwhoop is ever native to the prima donna.

The line between fiction and history is lightly drawn or completely erased in operatic plotting, but the following lead all the rest in popularity. There are thirty-two operas entitled *Columbus* and twenty-nine on Peru; most of the works on Pizarro are derived from Kotzebue's *Die Spanier in Peru.* Fernando Cortez and Ponce de León are the remaining heroes of the age of discovery. Twenty-three works stress the appeal of Mexico and, presumably, Montezuma. No North American subject, other than the Indian, has drawn so much attention, but Rip van Winkle claims seven works; there are five on Cooper's *The Last of the Mohicans,* and two from his lesser-known *The Spy.* In passing we may note that Cooper was among the ten most frequently translated authors from English into various foreign languages in the year 1958. Europeans, including the Russians, are reading Cooper long after Americans have done with him. Ten operas have been inspired by Longfellow's poems — *Hiawatha, Evangeline,* and *The Courtship of Miles Standish.* Six works were drawn from Hawthorne. Harriet Beecher Stowe leads Louisa May Alcott by a score of three to one in their best-known works. *Uncle Tom's Cabin (La Capanna dello zio Tom)* is admitted thrice, but rejected more often under suspicion of being too frivolously treated. Perhaps it is impossible to take that work seriously, even in opera.

* * * * *

There are many claims to being "first":

Columbus; or, The Discovery of America, by an anonymous author, was probably the first attempt to treat Columbus in terms of the theater. There is no reference to music.

The complete score for Bray's *The Indian Princess* was the first on an American subject to be published.

Bristow's *Rip van Winkle* was loudly proclaimed as the first American grand opera on an American subject, which might be qualified by "on a white subject and by an American citizen."

The first opera on an American subject to be produced in France was apparently Candeille's *Pizarro.*

Carnicer's *Cristóforo Colón* was the first opera on that subject by a Spanish composer.

Mary Carr Moore claims that *Narcissa* is the "first opera to be written, staged, and directed [conducted] by an American woman."

A very general designation is made with regard to Hawkins' *The Saw Mill* as "the first genuine American opera," the distinction depending on one's interpretation of the word "genuine."

Sonneck makes an equally subtle claim for Hopkinson's *The Temple of Minerva* as "our first attempt at 'grand opera'." He furthermore offers Andrew Bartón and James Ralph's *Disappointment; or, The Force of Credulity,* as "the first comic ballad opera produced by a native American."

There is no question about Lobo's *A Noite de São João* being "the first Brazilian opera in the Portuguese language," or Ortiz de Zárate's claim to have composed "the first opera by a Chilean composer performed in Chile."

Ottoboni's *Il Colombo* was the earliest Columbus opera, dating from 1690, and Hewitt's *Tammany* is claimed by Sonneck to be the "first Indian opera," which is true insofar as the title, indicating an Indian in the leading role, is concerned.

Vinatieri's *The American Volunteer* (c. 1889) is claimed as the first opera composed west of the Mississippi, but one must not forget Sobolewski's *Mohega,* composed in Milwaukee, only slightly to the east, thirty years earlier.

W. Franke Harling's *A Light from Saint Agnes* is said to be the first jazz opera produced in Europe.

Valle-Riestra's *Ollanta* was the first native Peruvian opera.

There are claims of priority from other aspects than these, but a few which one would like to encounter are missing, such as: an initial smash hit at the Metropolitan, a representative American subject made successful in opera houses of Europe, or a work which might grow in esteem, even from a small beginning, rather than (as is too often the case) one whose initial performance in the presence of social glitter is followed by critical disdain and oblivion.

* * * * *

Oscar G. Sonneck wrote in 1904:[7]

"Early American opera was an offspring of English ballad opera and hardly contained any promise for a truly national art. The nineteenth century has by no means improved the outlook. During the first quarter the melodrama thrived simultaneously with the senile ballad operas. Then the definite importance of Italian opera, inspired a few composers to boundless imitations of Rossini, Donizetti, Verdi, etc. Meyerbeer, Gounod, and finally Wagner, stood godfathers to the more modern American attempts at opera, and to-day we are as far from American opera of artistic importance as we ever have been. Not that our composers lack the power to write dramatic music, but our operatic life has been trimmed into a hot-house product.

"Whether or not a change for the better will take place, cannot be foretold. If not, then the task of the future historian of American opera will not be enviable, for he will have very little to say."

The past half-century illustrates dogged persistence on the part of our composers, coupled with general apathy on the part of audiences. The record of failure grows not only longer but more ominous, because many of the earlier works, though simple of circumstance, were fair successes. Sonneck writes from the point of view of opera by Americans, on whatever subject; the interest of this study concerns a smaller, but not more hopeful, segment of the total picture.

In the wake of scientific advances, subjects which formerly were purposely shielded as "apart," or ridiculed for the same reason, are now amenable to the arts. Experimental theater and the films are now grasping consequential ideas, while literature has revolutionized the very nature of language in order to convey abstract ideas of a modern age. Painting struggles with the same problems, breaking out of the restrictions of subject-matter and technique which ages have put upon it as literal representation or harmless fancy. The artist has gone far beyond the reach of the average citizen's ability to follow, but he has at the same time extended the frontiers of man's capacity to understand the infinite.

---

[7] Oscar G. Sonneck: *Early Opera in America* (New York: G. Schirmer, 1915).

Music is reacting last. But with opera — an extension of the literate stage and heretofore meekly bowing in compromise with its own boundless cosmology — opera may well find its particular transcendence more aptly suited to the conveyance of the universal than it has done in the admittedly limited and unsatisfactory areas of personal romance and grossly fictionalized historical re-creation.

No people has contributed more to the modern scientific age than have the North Americans. Is it not possible that the experimentation thus far so crudely attempted by a few of the avant-garde composers listed here, and the feeble earnestness of others unprepared for their task, may have the same significance for the future as the experiments in sound of Ussachevsky, Antheil, Varèse, and Cage?

The true potentialities of the American subject are man and the universe, and few subjects illustrating such broad concepts can be treated without reflecting in concrete measure the influence of American thought.

* * * * *

Are we nowadays able to find a common denominator in the future of the American repertory? As hitherto noted, opera in America has followed the general patterns of opera in Europe. Irving Kolodin asks this question relative to all opera composed by Americans, but his conclusions may well apply for the present to the narrower aspect of this volume's coverage. He considers that American operas are "best when they are unpretentious, unspectacular, and of modest scope. The grand gesture, the trumpets-on-the-stage of Verdi's *Aida* are as foreign to our native way of thinking and feeling as Porgy's 'Plenty O'Nuttin' would be in Tchaikovsky's *Pique Dame.*

"No doubt because the American way of singing and speaking came into its own through the 'musical,' in a line from Kern and Gershwin to Rodgers and Loesser, what sounds right and authentic to us in a more serious vein is best projected within the same physical dimensions (a City Center rather than a Metropolitan) with an orchestra not too much bigger. This is not to say that something bigger may not emerge, as manner becomes style and a way of performance is evolved from a performable repertory. But it must certainly develop out of modest beginnings rather than, as was the case in the period of Metropolitan Opera promotion of composers from Parker to Deems Taylor and Howard Hanson, and works from *Mona* to *Merry Mount,* being imposed on whatever talents were available." (*Saturday Review,* Oct. 28, 1961)

* * * * *

The alert reader has already made a clear distinction between *operas on American subjects* and *operas by Americans.* Anticipating a dozen or so examples, my innocence led me into a veritable forest of titles containing much dead wood. Rather than lose the forest for the trees by stressing evident virtues or ridiculing obvious faults, I have allowed those which appear to be unreclaimable failures their comfortable oblivion, only stopping to mark the tablet of memory with "Here lies." And yet who shall know with certainty which are dead and which are merely recumbent? With so little curiosity for them, we may not go beyond the barest generalizations as to their merits. As an aid to the reader a few works are mentioned which might appear as legitimate entries, but really are not so, for reasons given.

A few titles are here because there is no proof that they should be excluded. Captain Cook, Captain Kidd, and sometimes Robinson Crusoe are of doubtful operatic calibre, and I suspect that they were paraded for a few hours on a hinterland stage and gladly abandoned. They were apparently not seen in New York, or Odell would have caught them in his all-embracing net. I would admit Stearns' *The Bride of the Hudson* as a likely setting of *Sleepy Hollow,* were there evidence to prove it operatic; Thorne's *The Maid of Plymouth* might also qualify. Dates of first performance are those given by the painstaking Alfred Loewenberg or by Julius Mattfeld; I know of no better source for terminal dates than Nicolas Slonimsky's 1959 revision of *Baker's Biographical Dictionary of Musicians.*

The corpus of operatic materials is frightening to any modest researcher, and all thought of absolute finality in any musical subject becomes impossible in view of the fact that Dalayrac, for instance, wrote fifty-six operas, Gabrielli twenty-two, Ricci thirty, Majo twenty, and so on. This list, so hopefully prepared, can present only a fraction of the total.

Musicological surveys are impossible without the aid of colleagues and well-wishers. A number of contemporary composers have willingly provided information on work in progress; it is disconcerting that the younger have been far more responsive than the older. Victor Yellin has provided twenty-five titles of this list and offered useful information about others. Nicolas Slonimsky contributed a few unusual items and read part of the manuscript; he was also helpful many other ways. Gilbert Chase provided dates of South American composers and referred me to Mrs. Barbara Krader of the Pan American Union, who came to the rescue with further identifications. Oliver Daniel of Broadcast Music, Inc., and Judith Dvorkin of the American Composers Alliance, offered their contemporary records, and Gale McGovern read the manuscript with care. Ernst Krohn went to great pains to identify persons associated with the musical life of St. Louis, and William Lichtenwanger of the Library of Congress shook the dust from Joplin's *Treemonisha.* Public libraries in several cities added that support without which no arm of research can long remain strong. In particular, Daniel Koury, formerly of the Boston Public Library, should be thanked. Prof. Lawrence C. Wroth, emeritus head of the distinguished John Carter Brown Library at Brown University, suggested several early titles.

The most concentrated bodies of information on this topic are a chapter in Frederick H. Martens' *1001 Nights of Opera* and Edward Ellsworth Hipsher's *American Opera and Its Composers;* my work frequently owes its sense of direction to theirs, along with John Towers' *Dictionary-Catalogue of Operas.* The question marks, incomplete entries, and admitted frustrations await further enlightenment from whatever source.

You do look, my son, in a mov'd sort,
As if you were dismay'd; be cheerful, sir,
Our revels now are ended. These our actors,
As I foretold you, were all spirits and
Are melted into thin air, into thin air:
And, like the baseless fabric of this vision,
The cloud-capp'd towers, the gorgeous palaces,
The solemn temples, the great globe itself,
Yea, all which it inherit, shall dissolve
And, like this insubstantial pageant faded,
Leave not a rack behind. We are such stuff
As dreams are made on, and our little life
Is rounded with a sleep.

(Shakespeare: *The Tempest,* Act IV, Sc. 1)

OPERAS ON AMERICAN SUBJECTS

ANONYMOUS

The Cruelty of the Spaniards in Peru **London, 1658**

Text by Sir William Davenant (1606-1668), poet laureate from 1638 until his death. He also wrote *The Siege of Rhodes* (1656), with music by C. Coleman, G. Hudson, H. Lawes, H. Cooke, and Locke, which was the first English opera, although the term "opera" was not used. (Lawrence C. Wroth.) Strictly speaking, these works would not be called operas, but they were unquestionably musical plays.

ANONYMOUS

Columbus; or, The Discovery of America **Baltimore, March 21, 1783**

This tantalizing bit of information, exhumed by Sonneck, need not detain us. In all likelihood it represents a first, alarmingly prophetic attempt to memorialize Columbus in terms of the theater. Were there more information available, Sonneck would have found it, including a reference to music. See Ottoboni.

The accompanying *Harlequin's Revels* was "a new pantomine entertainment, being the *second* time of performance."

ANONYMOUS

May Day in Town; or, New York in an Uproar **New York, May 18, 1787**

Libretto by Royall Tyler in two acts. "Music compiled from the most eminent masters with an Overture and Accompaniments." (Sonneck)

This was a skit on a situation still with us — the much-dreaded May Day moving.

ANONYMOUS

Slave in Algiers; or, A Struggle for Freedom **Philadelphia, Dec. 22, 1794**

Verses by Susanna Haswell Rowson, actress, musician, proprietor of a finishing school for young ladies, and author of the best-selling novel *Charlotte Temple: A Tale of Virtue.*

The largest collection of materials on Mrs. Rowson is owned by C. Walter Barrett of Virginia.

ANONYMOUS

Americania and Elutheria; or, A New Tale of the Genii
Charleston, S.C., Feb., 1798

A "Musical and Allegorical Masque" whose plot defies condensation into less space than that given by Sonneck in his *Miscellaneous Studies* (pp. 85, 86). The Masque is performed for the benefit of a Hermit of the Allegani *(sic)* Mountains who is ignorant of the American Revolution. The popular star Mr. Placide was Chief of the Dancing Spirits, and Mrs. Placide was Chief of the Wood Nymphs. Neither author nor composer is known.

ANONYMOUS

Federation Triumphant in the Steady Hearts of Connecticut Alone; or, The Turnpike Road to a Fortune — **Hartford, c. 1801**

ANONYMOUS

The Story of Columbus

Published in New York by D. Longworth, 1803.

ANONYMOUS

Yankee Chronology; or, Huzza for the Constitution — **New York, 1812**

A musical interlude in one act, set in New York; text by William Dunlap, music probably gathered from several sources.

ADAM, ADOLPHE (1803 - 1856)

Les Mohicans — **Paris, 1837**

A ballet in two acts including Indians and the famous Leatherstocking of Cooper, Natty Bumpo. One critic wrote: "It would have been a pity to devote a valuable score to the grotesque gambols of a mob of Mohegan braves." (Martens)

ALBRIGHT, LOIS (1904 -)

Hopitu (Hopi People) — **New York, 1955**

Libretto by M. W. Billingsley in one act. Based on ancient Hopi legends and performed by a cast of full-blooded Hopi Indians with ceremonial dances. "Music score for first time incorporated Primitive Chants," the composer wrote on May 24, 1955. The concert performance in Carnegie Hall was directed from the piano. "Now in revision, being made into a three act opera . . . definitely an Opera and intended to be staged."

ALLEN, PAUL HASTINGS (1883 - 1952)

The Last of the Mohicans (L'Ultimo dei Moicani) **Florence, Feb. 24, 1916**

Three acts, based on James Fenimore Cooper, adapted by Zangarini. Scene in the region of Lake George, New York, about 1757; the cast includes Huron and Delaware Indians.

Orchestral and vocal scores published by Ricordi.

ANFOSSI, PASQUALE (1727 - 1797)

L'Americana in Olanda (The American in Holland) **Venice, 1778**

Two acts.

ANTHEIL, GEORGE (1900 - 1959)

Transatlantic; or, The People's Choice **Frankfurt, May 25, 1930**

35 scenes, including Childs Restaurant, lady's bath, and revolving doors. Time: 1920's. Composer librettist. The strong influence of Ernst Krenek, who spent four days examining the score, is acknowledged. The work is a political satire in which "an ambitious political demagogue shoots his way into the White House."

Vocal score published by Universal-Edition.

Antheil maintains that the work was a great success, citing twenty curtain calls, but claims that the impending shadow of Hitler was influencing German theaters to adopt a conservative policy in regard to new works. Ezra Pound, John Gunther, and a trainload of Antheil's Paris friends came for the première; a Russian critic liked the work, but said that it could not be produced in his country owing to the theme of general political elections.

The composer discusses his work at length in *Bad Boy of Music* (New York, Doubleday, 1945).

The Wish **Louisville, Ky., April 2, 1955**

Tragic opera in one act, libretto by the composer. Commissioned and performed by The Louisville Orchestra, Robert Whitney, Director. Four performances were given of a work having eight characters; the scene is Alberto's Cafe, "a few years ago" in Greenwich Village, New York. The work is recorded by The Louisville Orchestra, Moritz Bombard conducting.

APPLETON, ADELINE CAROLA (1886 -)

The Witches' Well **Tacoma, Wash., May, 1928**

Prologue and one act. Scene: Salem, 1692. Composer librettist with additional lyrics by Percy Davis. Story in Hipsher.

ARDITI, LUIGI (1822 - 1903)

La Spia — **New York, March 24, 1856**

Three acts; libretto by F. Manetta, based on James Fenimore Cooper's *The Spy.* It is explained that the Father of His Country is not brought on the stage in person from a feeling of reverence and respect. Story in Martens. This work was a success in its day; it is a tale of Harvey Birch, a spy dressed as pedlar, who brought information to General Washington. *Hail, Columbia* is used.

"Though its positive merit is not great, many a work in no way superior has been produced with considerable success at the principal theaters of Italy, and thought worthy of publication. The plot is not well selected. It lacks dramatic progress. Its power to interest depends entirely upon its association with Cooper's novel . . . Signor Arditi has made Donizetti his model in solos, while Verdi guides his pen in concerted music. It is not difficult to discern which composer he is seeking to emulate, and even to determine with some approach to accuracy the particular composition in the beauty of which he has found his inspiration." *(New York Courier & Enquirer)*

See Villani's work on the same subject.

ARNOLD, SAMUEL (1740 - 1802)

New Spain; or, Love in Mexico — **London, July 16, 1790**

Libretto by John Scawen.

Inkle and Yarico — **London, Aug. 4, 1787**

Words by G. Coleman, the younger, based on No. 11 of *The Spectator,* by Richard Steele. Part of the action takes place on shipboard, en route to America. An Indian, named Wowski, is dressed in leopard skins, and sings:

> Wampum, wampum, lenki manko powantowski,
> Black men plenty twenty fight for me.

AUBER, DANIEL-FRANÇOIS (1782 - 1871)

Manon Lescaut — **Paris (Opéra-Comique), Feb. 23, 1856**

Libretto by Augustin Eugène Scribe in three acts, after Prévost. Scene: Paris and (Act III) New Orleans.

Orchestral score published by Boieldieu, 1856; vocal score by St. Étienne, 1856. Critics considered Act III superior to the others.

BACON, ERNST (1898 -)

A Tree On the Plains — **Spartanburg, S. C., May 2, 1942**

Libretto by Paul Horgan published in *Southwest Review*, Dallas, Vol. 28, 1943. "No arias; plenty of songs; much declarative melody for dialogue; some crooning." Scene: on the plains of the Southwest.

BALFE, MICHAEL WILLIAM (1808 - 1870)

The Maid of Artois **London, May 27, 1836**

Words by Alfred Bunn, based on the story of Manon Lescaut by the Abbé Prévost. Acts II and III take place in Guiana.

For many years the identity of this opera was unknown. Riemann and Towers credited an opera *Manon,* composed in 1836, to Balfe, but the work could not be located. Printed scores, inasmuch as this work was in ballad-style, gave no clue to the location implied by the story. It was known that the work was expressly composed for Maria Malibran. In 1911 Miss Barbara Duncan, then of the Boston Public Library, located a collection of press notices from the first performance in London in 1836 with Anna Bishop. On the first page of the old volume was a clipping with the statement that (of the final scene) "it is no discredit to Mr. Bunn that he has borrowed it from the incomparable romance of *Manon Lescaut.*" Here was proof that Balfe's *Manon* and *The Maid of Artois* were one and the same opera.

BARBIERI, CARLO EMMANUELE DI (1822 - 1867)

Cristoforo Colombo **Berlin, Dec. 26, 1848**

BARBIERI, FRANCISCO ASENJO (1823 - 1894)

Robinson Crusoe **Milan, 1881**

An "operetta semi-fantastica" in three acts.

BATTISTA, VINCENZO (1823 - 1873)

Il Corsaro della Guadalupa **Naples, 1853**

BEACH, L.

Jonathan Postfree; or, The Honest Yankee **New York, 1807**

A ballad opera of which Beach may be the author rather than the composer.

BEESON, JACK (1931 -)

Hello Out There New York, July, 1954

Chamber opera in one act adapted from a play by William Saroyan.

Scene: Jail in a small Texas town. Duration, 40 minutes. There are five singing parts. Vocal score published by Mills Music.

"Beeson's work stood out because the score indicated exceptional gifts on the part of the composer in the difficult field of operatic composition." *(Musical America,* July 1954)

"With his small cast and orchestra, Beeson packs in *Hello Out There* a maximum of emotional contrast and dramatic action." (*Notes,* Sept. 1961)

The Sweet Bye and Bye New York, 1957

Libretto in two acts by Kenward Elmslie. Subject: Revivalism in Arkansas.

BENNETT, ROBERT RUSSELL (1894 -)

Maria Malibran New York, April 8, 1935

Libretto in three acts by Robert A. Simon. Scene: New York in 1825. Produced with success at the Juilliard School, with Josephine Antoine singing the title role.

BENOIST, FRANÇOIS (1794 - 1878)

Nisida; ou, les Amazons des Açores Paris, 1846

Columbus' final point of departure; an episode of the conquest of the Azores by the Portuguese.

BERNERS, LORD (1883 - 1950)

Le Carrosse du Saint-Sacrement Monte Carlo, 1923

Book after Mérimée, based on the story of La Périchole. One act. Performed on April 24, 1924, in Paris. Vocal score published by J. & W. Chester, Ltd., c. 1923. Entire score revised, 1926.

BERNSTEIN, LEONARD (1918 -)

Trouble in Tahiti Waltham, Mass., June 12, 1952

One act. First performed at the Brandeis University Festival of Creative Arts.

BERUTTI, ARTURO (1862 - 1938)

Pampa **Buenos Aires, July 27, 1897**

Libretto by G. Borra in three acts. Berutti's first opera on a national Argentine subject.

Yupanky **Buenos Aires, July 25, 1899**

An Inca opera in three acts with Spanish text by E. Rodríguez Larreta. The title role was sung by Enrico Caruso.

BEZANSON, PHILIP (1916 -)

Golden Child (Orig. *Western Child*) **Iowa City, July 28, 1959**

Libretto by Paul Engle in three acts. Performed at the State University of Iowa. An adaptation of the Nativity story set in Sutter's Fort during the Gold Rush. "A child is born in a manger, bringing peace and love to a group of gold-crazed miners and their gold-digging girl friends." *(New York Times)*

Selected by the Hallmark Hall of Fame for television presentation, Christmas 1960, offering a cast comprising Patricia Neway, Brenda Lewis, Jerome Hines, and Stephen Douglass, Herbert Grossman conducting.

BIMBONI, ALBERTO (1882 - 1960)

Winona **Portland, Ore., Nov. 11, 1926**

Libretto by Perry Williams in three acts. An Indian subject, employing Chippewa melodies, sung in unison. Cast included members of the Sioux-Dacotah tribes. This brings into question Lois Albright's statement regarding *Hopitu.* Story in Hipsher. Produced by the American Grand Opera Company, composer conducting; in 1928, performed in Minneapolis before an audience of 9,000 persons.

In the Name of Culture **Rochester, N. Y., 1949**

A chamber opera in one act, libretto by Norma Frizelle Stolzenbach. Satire on a "cultural" women's club session.

BISHOP, SIR HENRY ROWLEY (1786 - 1855)

Cortez; or, The Conquest of Mexico **London, 1823**

Historical drama in three acts, libretto by J. R. Planché. Vocal score published by Goulding, D'Almaine & Co., 1823.

The Virgin of the Sun **London, 1812**

Based on Kotzebue's *Die Spanier in Peru.*

BLAKESLEE, E. EARLE

The Legend of Wiwaste **Ontario, Calif., 1927**

Based on a Dacotah legend; utilizes Indian dances and melodies.

BLITZSTEIN, MARC (1905 - 1964)

Regina **Boston, Oct. 11, 1949**

Based on Lillian Hellman's successful play *The Little Foxes* and first sung on Broadway. Revised and mounted by the City Center Opera Company on April 2, 1953. Three acts. Vocal score published in New York by Chappell, c. 1954.

Blitzstein's one-act opera *The Cradle Will Rock,* originally produced on Broadway on June 16, 1937, was revived at the New York City Center in 1960. "My main objection to the appearance of the work in the New York City Opera's repertoire, however, is that it is not by any stretch of the aesthetic definition an opera, and therefore ought to have been left to Broadway (if Broadway wants it), since the resources of a fine operatic-repertory company are completely wasted in its presentation." (Winthrop Sargeant in *The New Yorker*)

BOERO, FELIPE (1884 -)

Tucumán **Buenos Aires, June 29, 1918**

A Spanish-American subject.

Raquela **Buenos Aires, June 25, 1923**

A Spanish-American subject; one act.

BONICIOLI, FRUHMAN RICARDO (1853 - 1933)

Don Juan de Garay **Buenos Aires, 1900**

Based on the life of a hero-founder of Argentina.

BONNER, EUGENE (1889 -)

Barbara Frietchie

Based on a play by Clyde Fitch; apparently not produced. Considered for production by the Paris Opéra-Comique, according to Hipsher, but rejected because the subject was too American to appeal to continental audiences. Composed about 1920.

BOTTESINI, GIOVANNI (1821 - 1889)

Cristoforo Colombo **Havana, Jan. 31, 1847**

Libretto in one act by Ramon de Palma. Three singers only, of which Columbus is a baritone. Arditi's *Reminiscences* make no mention of the work, and Bottesini's memoirs merely state that it was written in Spanish. There is fuller discussion in Tolón and Gonzáles, Chapter III, where the work is referred to as *Colón en Cuba.*

BRAGA, FRANCISCO (1868 - 1945)

Jupira **Rio de Janeiro, March 20, 1899**

Libretto by Doria, in one act. Set in the forest of Brazil about 1800. Vocal score published by Casa Guarany, J. Santos & Co., 1900.

BRAHAM, JOHN (1774 - 1856)

The Americans **London, 1811**

Braham was a tenor; his contracts always gave him the right to compose music for his own parts, if he so chose. See Matthew Peter King for further details.

BRAND, MAX (1896 -)

Maschinist Hopkins **Duisberg, April 13, 1929**

Prologue and three acts; text by the composer. This work in three acts is American by implication only. Several characters are distinct American types, jazz is used, and the design of one set strongly resembled the American flag. George Antheil made an English translation of the words, but it was also sung in Czech, Swedish, and Ukrainian. Vocal score published by Universal-Edition, 1928.

BRANDL, JOHANN (1835 - 1913)

Die Mormonen **Vienna, Nov. 22, 1879**

Libretto in three acts by A. Klischnegg and the composer. As in Dudley Buck's *Deseret,* this work makes comedy of the Mormon and his many wives. See also *Deseret* by Leonard Kastle.

BRAY, JOHN (1782 - 1822)

The Indian Princess; or, La Belle Sauvage **Philadelphia, April 6, 1808**

Libretto by J. Nelson Barker in three acts. For full discussion of this work, see the excellent article by H. Wiley Hitchcock in *Notes,* Vol. XII, No. 3 (June 1955).

Barker describes his work as an opera, and all the music for the original version was published (Philadelphia, G. E. Blake, 1808). Seldom in these days was so elaborate a score published in its entirety. Mr. Hitchcock's article gives copious examples of the music, including part of the Overture with its 178 measures in C minor! There are airs, duets, and a Finale. Barker was at least chronologically faithful to the historic account of Captain John Smith and Pocahontas, while Bray proves himself competent, if not superior to others of his time, in giving this melodrama operatic form in the manner exemplified by Mozart, Salieri, and Rossini.

BRISTOW, GEORGE F. (1825 - 1898)

Rip van Winkle **New York (Niblo's Garden), Sept. 27, 1855**

Libretto in three acts by Jonathan Howard Wainwright, subsequently revised by others. The first American grand opera on an American subject.

Wainwright was a military man who showed his predilection for marches and spectacle, the soldier's chorus and drills. Critics considered that this sort of thing slowed up the action and recommended that the four-hour work be cut. Rip was absent for an entire act, and the love story was carried on for too long a time.

Subject, author, composer, and librettist were American, but it would be too much to expect that a native stamp would show in the music. J. S. Dwight considered that Bristow missed important dramatic opportunities but did well with set pieces, and with songs. The orchestration was deemed inexpert, with brass overpowering strings or sounding too thin other than in places where it was too loud. The orchestra was "lifeless and devoid of that brilliance we must meet in all modern operas," Dwight wrote, mindful of Meyerbeer, Verdi, and the early Wagner which he had recently heard for the first time.

"Probably Longfellow or Willis would have done better, but then, no one expects poets to write librettos; such drudgery is left to verse-makers. The work is not properly a grand opera for much of the dialogue is spoken, a shabby practise which I hope may go out of fashion. The melodies are light, resembling those of Auber, sometimes reminding one of the better class of native compositions by some miscalled Ethiopian. Simple, graceful themes set in strongly marked rhythms keep the public feet in motion, and the public heart pounding with delight." (Letter to *Dwight's Journal of Music*)

Rip van Winkle is a bass; Louisa Pyne, a popular favorite of the day, sang the part of Peterkee.

The work was revived in Philadelphia in 1870.

"The sum and substance of Mr. Bristow's production may be simply stated. As a musical composition it is a study in a hard-beaten track, evincing scholarship but being decidedly weak in color, and wanting in terse melody. Perhaps the best we can say of it is that it presents prettiness in lieu of poetic thought.

"The voice is an organ for which Mr. Bristow shows small partiality. . . Granting that his style is inoffensive, it is still not to be commended for stage purposes. It is in a general way feeble and aimless, void of clear sentiment, and innocent of poetic fancies."

See article by Waldemar Reich: "When Bristow's 'Rip' was Sung at Niblo's Garden." (*Musical America,* Vol. 43, No. 7)

BUCHAROFF, SIMON (1881 - 1955)

The Lover's Knot **Chicago, Jan. 15, 1916**

Libretto by Cora Bennett Stevenson. Set in Norfolk, Virginia, about 1870. Story in Martens. One performance.

BUCK, DUDLEY (1839 - 1909)

Deseret; or, A Saint's Affliction **New York, Oct. 11, 1880**

An unpublished comic opera in three acts, with libretto by William A. Crofutt, set to music by a famous composer of religious music. Critics found the score too churchly and disapproved of the Mormon theme. See entries under Brandl and Kastle.

Buck's *Paul Revere's Ride* and *The Voyage of Columbus* are cantatas.

CADMAN, CHARLES WAKEFIELD (1881 - 1946)

Daoma; or, Land of Misty Water

Unproduced "Indian Idyl" in four acts with libretto by Nelle Richmond Eberhart, after a story by Francis La Flesche (an Omaha Indian). Composed in 1912 but never orchestrated. This work is sometimes referred to as *Ramala.*

Shanewis; or, The Robin Woman **New York, March 23, 1918**

Libretto in two acts by Nelle Richmond Eberhart. First produced at the Metropolitan and revived on Dec. 5, 1924 in Denver, Colorado. Vocal score published by Morris (White-Smith), 1918.

The story concerns an Indian girl who falls in love with the son of her benefactress, engaged to another.

The Sunset Trail **Denver, Dec. 5, 1922**

An "operatic contata," with libretto in two scenes by Nelle Richmond Eberhart. Also produced in Chicago by the Civic Opera Company under the direction of Mary Garden. Vocal score published by Theodore Presser, 1922. The story deals with the forcible removal of a western Indian tribe to a reservation under the supervision of United States troopers.

A Witch of Salem **Chicago, Dec. 8, 1926**

Libretto in two acts by Nelle Richmond Eberhart. Story in Hipsher.

CANDEILLE, PIERRE JOSEPH (1744 - 1827)

Pizarre; ou, la Conquête du Pérou **Paris, 1785**

"Tragédie-Lyrique en cinq Actes; Représentée pour la première Fois, par l'Academie-Royale de Musique, le Mardi 3 Mai 1785." On the verso of the title-page: "Les Paroles sont de M.***"

This is apparently the earliest work of its kind. Brown University Library (Providence, Rhode Island) has a copy of the words only. (Information supplied by Lawrence C. Wroth.)

CAREY, HENRY (1687 - 1743)

True Blue **New York, 180-**

A ballad opera based on *Nancy; or, The Parting Lovers,* changed to include a scene at the Battery (Sonneck). *Nancy* was produced in England in 1739.

CARLSON, CHARLES F. (1875 -)

The Courtship of Miles Standish

Libretto in two acts by the composer, based on Longfellow's poem. Apparently not produced.

Hester; or, The Scarlet Letter

Libretto by the composer based on Hawthorne. Apparently not produced.

CARNICER, RAMÓN (1789 - 1855)

Cristóforo Colón **Madrid, Jan. 12, 1831**

Libretto in two acts by Felice Romani. This appears to be the first *Columbus* opera by a Spanish composer, and is said to be the composer's best work. It was produced in Havana also in 1831. See opera to the same libretto by Morlacchi.

CARTER, ELLIOTT (1908 -)

Tom and Lily

An uncompleted work, withdrawn and destroyed by the composer. (Letter of Dec. 1957.) Composed in 1934.

CARTER, ERNEST TROW (1866 - 1953)

The Blonde Donna; or, The Fiesta of Santa Barbara — **New York, Feb., 1931**

Comic opera in three acts, suitable for production by amateurs. Libretto by the composer. The initial performance was in concert form at the Century Theater; the first stage production was in Brooklyn, on Dec. 8, 1931. Vocal score published by The Composers Press, c.1936.

The White Bird — **Chicago, March 6, 1924**

Libretto in one act by Brian Hooker, with scene in Adirondack lake district early in the 19th century. It is not an Indian opera. The first concert performance was given in New York on May 23, 1922, composer conducting. Story in Martens. Libretto published by Yale University Press, 1924.

CARVALHO, ELEAZAR DE (1912 -)

Descuberta do Brasil — **Rio de Janeiro, June 18, 1939**

Libretto in two acts by Barras.

Tiradentes (literally, tooth-puller) — **Rio de Janeiro, Sept. 7, 1941**

The title is the nickname of a hero of the Brazilian Revolution, who was a dentist. Work produced on Independence Day.

CASE, HENRY LINCOLN

Hinotito: A Romance of Love and Politics

A comic opera (possibly beyond the scope of this listing) with libretto by Frederic W. Pangborn, composed about 1922 but probably not produced.

CASELLA, DONNA FELICITA

Cristoforo Colombo — **Nice, 1865**

No further information.

CASTRO, HERRERA RICARDO (1864 - 1907)

Atzimba — **Mexico City, Nov. 9, 1900**

Based on the conquest of Michoacán.

CHADWICK, GEORGE WHITEFIELD (1854 - 1931)

The Padrone

Libretto in two acts by D. E. Stevens. Stevens was a lawyer become musical enthusiast and member of the firm of C. C. Birchard, music publishers; he wrote librettos for others, including Henry Hadley.

In the late 19th century, in the days of Italian and Irish immigration, the padrone symbolized that which was corrupt in human relationships. It was he who financed the importation of poorer men and, to a lesser extent, women, contracted them to work in payment of their passage, controlled housing, boarding, clothing and, in fact, held them in virtual peonage for years. Chadwick considered that the situation had sociological merit for expression in opera, as did his colleague, Frederick S. Converse, who wrote *The Immigrants* at about the same time.

The four principals sing in Italian, others in English; the two scenes are in a restaurant and on the wharf where a ship has arrived from the homeland. The leading female role is that of a tambourine girl who accompanies an organ-grinder on the streets. The work was begun on February, 1912, and finished in vocal score during December; it was orchestrated for large ensemble in the months following. The manuscript score is in the library of the New England Conservatory of Music.

Chadwick's musical method "is based on the union of Wagner's symphonic recitative and Italian lyricism first used extensively by Verdi in *Otello,*" writes Victor Yellin. The orchestra's dramatic role is minor in arias and ensembles, but predominant in the extended interlude between acts. There is no overture.

A perfunctory note, returning the manuscript from the Metropolitan, stated that it was "not found suitable for production at their establishment." Private report stated that Gatti-Casazza did not like a theme having to do with humble Italians, *Cavalleria* notwithstanding.

See the very complete discussion of this work in *The Life and Operatic Works of George Whitefield Chadwick,* by Victor Yellin, Harvard University Dissertation, 1957 (unpublished).

Concert selections were performed in Carnegie Hall, Dec. 6, 1961 by the Orchestra of America, Richard Korn, conductor.

Mr. Chadwick's *Rip van Winkle* is an Overture.

CIMAROSA, DOMENICO (1749 - 1801)

Le Vergine del sole — St. Petersburg, Nov. 6, 1789

A Peruvian subject with libretto in three acts by F. Moretti.

This work was produced in Bologna and Madrid the following year.

CLAFLIN, AVERY (1898 -)

Hester Prynne — Hartford, Conn., Dec. 15, 1934

Based on Hawthorne's "The Scarlet Letter." In three acts.

One scene only was produced.

COERNE, LOUIS ADOLPHE (1870 - 1922)

A Woman of Marblehead **Buffalo, N. Y., 189-**

A work in two acts, composed in 1897. Coerne gave a concert performance in Buffalo. Orchestral excerpts were played in New York, 1907. Deals with Floyd Ireson, who was unjustly punished by the women of Marblehead.

COLBURN, GEORGE (1878 - 1921)

The Masque of Montezuma

An Aztec subject, this work was composed in 1913; apparently unproduced.

COLE, ROSSETTER GLEASON (1866 - 1952)

The Maypole Lovers

Libretto by Carty Ranck. Composed 1919-1931, but not produced. The subject is Merry Mount, near Quincy, Massachusetts. An orchestral suite was played in Chicago on Jan. 9, 1936.

CONVERSE, FREDERICK S. (1871 - 1940)

The Immigrants

Libretto in three acts by Percy Mackaye, commissioned for the Boston Opera Company, but not produced. Composed in 1914. Scene: New York in the early 20th century. The story is given in Martens; the score is in possession of the New England Conservatory of Music, Boston. This is a most interesting work, deserving of further attention.

The Sacrifice **Boston, March 3, 1911**

The composer made his own libretto in three acts, drawing on a story by Lt. H. A. Wise. Lyrics are by John A. Macy. The scene is California about 1846, with Indians, Mexicans, and Spaniards. Vocal score published by H. W. Gray. The story is in Martens.

COPLAND, AARON (1900 -)

The Tender Land **New York (City Center), April 1, 1954**

Libretto in two acts by Horace Everett.

"Mr. Copland remains constantly on the brink of his own especial brand of greatness without taking the final plunge to bring this greatness to us. What the composer has succeeded in doing, however, is to create a genuine atmosphere piece that breathes, smells, even feels like the Mid-West. It is gentle, homespun, sweet, and casual." *(New York Times)*

Two drifters arrive at a farm on the eve of a high-school graduation dance. One falls in love with the girl. In the morning his buddy takes him away and the girl is left with the realization that she must leave home and "break the pattern" of farm life to assert her own being in a larger world.

The work was sung on August 2, 1954, at "Tanglewood," summer home of the Boston Symphony Orchestra, in a revised version. Orchestral excerpts were made into a Suite (1959). Vocal score published by Boosey & Hawkes, 1956.

Copland's *The Second Hurricane* (1937) is a "play-opera for school performance," set in the Middle West. It was first sung in New York, April 21, 1937.

COPPOLA, PIETRO ANTONIO (1793 - 1877)

Cristoforo Colombo

Composed about 1854.

DALAYRAC, NICOLAS (1753 - 1809)

Azémia, ou, Le nouveau Robinson — Fontainebleau, Oct. 17, 1786

Libretto in three acts by Lachabeaussière. Scene: Pacific island near American shore, involving English, Spanish, and Indians. Azémia is the daughter of an Englishman who lives in the primitive conditions of Robinson Crusoe. Following adventures with a Spanish sea captain and with native savages, Azémia weds another island white, Prosper. English and Spanish sailors provide the chorus.

A new third act was written, the title changed to *Azémia; ou, Les Sauvages,* and a Paris production given on May 3, 1787. New York heard the work on Sept. 20, 1827.

DAMROSCH, WALTER (1862 - 1950)

The Dove of Peace — Philadelphia, Oct. 15, 1912

A comic opera, with book by Wallace Irwin, but produced with an orchestra of fifty pieces and a cast featuring singers from the Metropolitan Opera. Scenes include Portsmouth, New Hampshire, the United States Senate Chamber, and Guam Island. It is described as "a satire on the dream of universal peace," in which the Spanish Governor-General of Guam does not know that his country and the United States are at war. When a volley is fired by an American ship, he sends a polite word that he is fresh out of gunpower and will not be able to return the salute until supplies arrive in a month's time.

Vocal score published by G. Schirmer, 1912.

The Man without a Country **New York, May 12, 1937**

Libretto in two acts by Arthur Guiterman, from the story by Edward Everett Hale. To the cast of characters, which includes Aaron Burr and Stephen Decatur, a woman, given the name of Mary Rutledge, is added. In Hale's story Philip Nolan lives to old age, but the libretto requires his early death as a hero.

Produced in the spring season of the Metropolitan Opera, with the composer conducting; Helen Traubel sang there for the first time, the evening of the première "marking the apogee of Mr. Damrosch's career," according to Lawrence Gilman.

Vocal score published by G. Schirmer, 1937.

The Scarlet Letter **Boston, Feb. 10, 1896**

Libretto in three acts, based on the novel of Nathaniel Hawthorne by George Parsons Lathrop, Hawthorne's son-in-law. Scenes include Long Wharf, Boston, and School and State Streets at a time when the population of the city numbered fewer than one thousand persons.

First sung in concert form (1895) at Carnegie Hall, New York, with Nordica and Campanari, a chorus of four hundred voices, and the New York Symphony Orchestra. The balconies were filled, but there were empty seats in the lower parts of the hall. The first full New York production, following that in Boston, was on March 6, 1896. Johanna Gadski sang the role of Hester.

Anton Seidl dubbed the work a "New England Nibelung Trilogy," and Mr. Damrosch, in *My Musical Life,* looked back on it as showing talent, but bearing too definite a stamp of his Wagnerian predilections.

DAVID, FÉLICIEN (1810 - 1876)

La Perle du Brésil **Paris, Nov. 22, 1851**

Opéra-comique in three acts by J. Gabriel and Sylvain Saint-Étienne. Scenes are in the Portuguese court, mid-ocean, and the forest of Brazil.

Jaquarita, or Zora for short, is an Indian girl captured by a Spanish naval officer who takes her back to Europe with the idea of baptizing and marrying her. But Jaquarita, or Zora for short, falls in love with a young man not of officer calibre, and the two endeavor to sail back to Brazil on the next voyage. The ship is wrecked on the Brazilian coast, and all hands are captured by Indians. The entire cast is at the point of massacre by the Indians when Jaquarita volunteers the national anthem of her people and proves that she is the long-lost daughter of their deceased chieftain. See also the opera by Jacques Halévy on the same mélange.

There is some confusion as to whether the lady's name is spelled "Jaq" or "Jag".

The plot is similar to that of *L'Africaine.* The music is considered David's best, but unusually symphonic for its time.

A great success was achieved in 1883 when the work was revived for the Paris début of the American singer Emma Nevada (Wixom).

Vocal score published by Launer, 1851.

The composer's *Christophe Colomb; ou, le découverte du Nouveau monde* is a symphonic ode.

DAVIES, JOHN

The Forest Rose; or, The American Farmers **New York, Oct. 7, 1825**

Two acts. This work introduced the character of Brother Jonathan Ploughboy at Chatham Gardens, and included the song, "The Old Oaken Bucket," composed by Samuel Woodworth.

Italian Opera, sung by the Garcia troupe, opened on Nov. 29, 1825, destroying much of the active interest in works of a native genre, and diverting American taste to the sophistications of continental life.

Revived in New York in 1849 and 1855.

DAVIS, A. J.

The Last of the Mohicans

De CAMPOS, CARLOS (1866 - 1927)

Un Caso Singolare **São Paulo and Rio de Janeiro, 1926**

Libretto in three acts by Cardin.

De KOVEN, REGINALD (1859 - 1920)

Rip van Winkle **Chicago, Jan. 2, 1920**

Libretto in three acts by Percy Mackaye. Also performed in New York on Jan. 30, 1920.

Mackaye added much detail to enrich the action. Rip has forgotten that he is to be married and makes his entrance with a group of children, flying a kite. He tells the children about the legend of Hendrick Hudson and his crew, and that every twenty years they return in a ghostly ship *Half Moon* to hold a party in the mountains. At that moment Hudson returns in a sunshine shower and his crew, not of elves as Irving portrays them, is a hard-drinking lot of sailor-men. Rip is accompanied to the mountains by the child Peterkee, but she returns to the village while Rip is being lulled to sleep. On his return, Rip does not marry Katrina, as in Irving's tale, but Peterkee, who has grown up during his twenty-year absence.

In the original production Georges Baklanoff (baritone) sang the role of Rip, and Evelyn Herbert made her début as Peterkee. Alexander Smallens conducted three performances.

Vocal score published by G. Schirmer, 1919.

De LEONE, FRANCESCO B. (1887 - 1948)

Alglala **Akron, Ohio, May 23, 1924**

Libretto by Cecil Fanning on an Indian subject. Story in Martens. Mabel Garrison and Edward Johnson sang this work in Akron, Cleveland, and New York. Vocal score published by G. Schirmer, 1924.

DELIUS, FREDERICK (1862 - 1934)

Koanga **Elberfeld, Germany, March 30, 1904**

Prologue, three acts, and epilogue. Libretto by C. F. Keary, drawn from George W. Cable's novel *The Grandissimes.* The composer was dissatisfied with Keary's work, and removed the English, leaving only his wife's German words. *Koanga* was produced in London in 1922; also in 1935, with the original English text, revised by Sir Thomas Beecham and Edward Agate.

Vocal score published by Boosey & Hawkes, c. 1935.

Setting: Louisiana, early 19th century. The Spanish slave-masters look forward to the arrival of Koanga, an African chieftain, as a new slave. His spirit is unbreakable, but they feel that Palmyra, an octoroon, may act as a Delilah in bringing him to accept his bondage. Koanga takes to the jungle with other slaves, and invokes Voodoo and black magic, bringing fire and ruin upon the plantation and himself.

"In *Koanga* Delius revelled in the colour and emotion of contrasted pictures, in tom-toms, Voodoo spells, the laughing choruses and wedding preparations." (Arthur Hutchings: *Delius,* London, 1949)

DELLO JOIO, NORMAN (1913 -)

Blood Moon **San Francisco, Sept. 18, 1961**

Grand opera in three acts (five scenes) with libretto by Gale Hoffman and the composer, set in New Orleans, New York, and Paris during the American Civil War. The problem is racial.

This work, originally commissioned by the Academy of Vocal Arts in Philadelphia, was first performed by the San Francisco Opera Association under a grant from the Ford Foundation.

DIBDIN, CHARLES (1745 - 1814)

The Quaker **London, May 3, 1775**

No definite locale is specified in this work, but it is possible, according to Sonneck, that it had a native air wherever produced. The libretto "as played in Boston" was published by Blake and Clapp in 1794; the work was heard in Philadelphia in October and in New York in December of the same year. Sonneck remarks upon the speed with which London successes were imported and notes from contemporary sources that the quality of production in America was equal to that abroad.

The Padlock London, Oct. 3, 1768

Text by I. Bickerstaffe, founded on Cervantes' *El Celoso extremeño.* Also produced in New York May 29, 1769. The composer created the part of Mungo, a Negro, not necessarily an American Negro.

DONIZETTI, GAETANO (1797 - 1848)

Il Furioso nell' Isola di San Domingo Rome, Jan. 2, 1833

Libretto in two acts by J. Ferretti, based on an episode from Cervantes' *Don Quixote.* Sung in Mexico and Havana in 1836, but apparently not in the United States.

Vocal score published by Launer, 184-.

DUSSEK, JAN LADISLAV (1760 - 1812)

Pizarro London, May 24, 1799

Incidental music for Sheridan's play, aided by Michael Kelly and others. (See Kelly.)

EAMES, HENRY PURMORT (1872 - 1950)

Priscilla

Comic opera based on Longfellow's *The Courtship of Miles Standish* with libretto by Hartley Burr Alexander, composed about 1920 and privately performed.

EDWARDS, JULIAN (1856 - 1910)

The Patriot

Tragic opera in one act with libretto by Stanislaus Stange. Vocal score (51pp.) published by M. Witmark, 1907. There is no record of a performance. There are six characters, including George Washington, a bass.

Edwards' other operas, including *When Johnny Comes Marching Home* (Detroit, Oct. 6, 1902) are light, romantic works, in the vein of those by De Koven, Herbert, and Sullivan; they were produced by the Whitney Light Opera Company with Broadway casts. Only in the finale to *Johnny* did Mr. Edwards approach an operatic standard.

EDWARDS, ROBERT

Tennessee **St. Louis, 1894**

A light opera.

EGK, WERNER (1901 -)

Christopher Columbus **Frankfurt, Jan. 13, 1942**

An "opera-oratorio" in three acts with libretto by the composer. Written as oratorio for radio in 1932 (Munich, July 13, 1933), and performed as an opera in 1942; revised in 1957. Indians in the cast sing to the extent of outlining an E-flat minor chord with simple harmonic accompaniment.

Vocal score published (reproduced from manuscript) by B. Schott's Söhne, c. 1942.

Die Verlobung in San Domingo **Munich, Nov. 27, 1963**

Opera in two acts with libretto based on novella by Kleist. Deals with the struggle of the Haitians against French rule in early 19th century.

Produced during the opening week at the rebuilt National Theater.

ENNA, EMIL (1877 - 1951)

The Dawn of the West **Portland, Ore., 1915**

Libretto in four acts by Freda Gratke. The composer was a nephew of August Enna.

FABRIZI, VINCENZO (1765 -)

Il Colombo **Rome, 1789**

FAETKENHAUER, MAX (c.1870 - 1940)

Amelia Mora **Cleveland, 1901**

Libretto by Gus Heege with scenes in Sweden and in a Wisconsin logging camp. Though intended to be an opera, critics considered that with pruning and editing it might make a satisfactory musical comedy.

FALLA, MANUEL de (1876 - 1946)

La Atlántida **Barcelona, Nov. 24, 1961**

This work was completed by Ernesto Halffter. It is based on an idea by the

Catalan writer Mose Jacinto Verdaguer (1845-1902) concerning Columbus and the westward movement. (See the *New York Times,* Mar. 16, 1958.) Sung in concert by cast of Metropolitan Opera singers at Philharmonic Hall, New York, on Sept. 29, 1962, under direction of Ernest Ansermet.

FANCIULLI, FRANCESCO ROGERS (1850 - 1915)

Priscilla; or, The Maid of Plymouth — **Norfolk, Va., Nov. 1, 1901**

Based on *The Courtship of Miles Standish* by Longfellow.

Malinche; or, The Day of Sacrifice

Based on Lew Wallace's novel *The Fair God,* dealing with the conquest of Mexico. Unproduced.

FARNER, EUGENE ADRIAN (1888 -)

The White Buffalo Maiden — **Boise, Idaho, April 26, 1923**

Libretto by Alfred Grubb. A Western Indian music-play in one act, dealing with the Sioux and utilizing Indian melodies.

FAVA, ALESSANDRO

Il Colombo — **Bologna, 1875**

This work was privately produced.

FERNÂNDEZ, OSCAR LORENZO (1897 - 1948)

Malazarte — **Rio de Janeiro, Sept. 30, 1941**

Three acts, Portuguese libretto (in an Italian translation) by Graça Aranha, dealing with legendary black magic, and taking place in Colonial Brazil. The composed conducted the world première.

FERRARI-TRECATE, LUIGI (1885 -)

La Capanna dello zio Tom — **Parma, Jan. 17, 1953**

Opera in three acts, libretto by E. Anceschi, after *Uncle Tom's Cabin* by Harriet Beecher Stowe, the work had one performance in Parma, but was revived at the Rome Opera House in March 1963.

"This is a story about good and bad niggers," said the English translation of program notes supplied for tourists. It was a story about Zio Tom, Signor Legree and Piccola Eva, a story about slavery in harsh old Kentucky. The première production celebrated the centenary of Lincoln's Emancipation Proclamation. "A great opera and a great story," shouted *Il Messaggero.* "The fight for freedom belongs to eternity, and where could it be better fought than on the stage of the Rome Opera House?" See article in *Time,* March 22, 1963.

Signor Ferrari-Trecate is quoted as saying: "My entire knowledge of American music is from the gramophone records I listened to in Parma . . . I have been to America only in my dreams. I will be happy if my opera is produced again, but I must admit that my greatest ambition is to write music for the films of Walt Disney."

FERREIRA, D. (1830 - 1916)

Columbus

Two acts, unproduced. The composer was Brazilian.
See also Florio and Giorza.

FINK, MYRON (1933 -)

Jeremiah — **Binghamton, N. Y., May 25, 1962**

Opera in six scenes with libretto by Mrs. Fink and Earlene Hawley, set in Illinois farm country in the 1880's. The story is that of a religious fanatic who kills his son. Produced at Harpur College.

Susanna and the Elders — **Vienna, 1955**

Presented while the composer was in Vienna on a Fulbright grant. See also opera on same subject by Floyd.

FIORAVANTI, VINCENZO (1799 - 1877)

Colombo alla scoperta delle Indie — **Naples, 1829**

Composed about 1828. Vocal score published in Milan by Lucca, 183-.

La Conquista del Messico — **Naples, 1829**

Robinson Crusoe — **Naples, 1828**

Composed about 1825.

FLORIDIA, PIETRO (1860 - 1932)

La Colonia libera — **Rome, May 7, 1899**

Libretto in four acts by Luigi Illica, based on a story *M'Liss* by Bret Harte. Scene: Mexico, early in the 19th century.

Sung in Cincinnati on Aug. 29, 1910, and in New York (abridged) on March 21, 1920, in English translation.

This work was well received in Italy. "The love scene in the forest, in the third act, aroused real enthusiasm." (Foreign correspondent, *New York Times.)*

Vocal score published by Ricordi, 1900.

Floridia's *Paoletta* is not an Indian opera.

The Scarlet Letter

Composed in 1902; apparently not produced. Submitted to the Metropolitan Opera during the Conried directorship (1903-1908).

FLORIO, CARYL (1843 - 1920)

Uncle Tom's Cabin — Philadelphia, 1882

Opera seria in five acts with libretto by H. Wayne Ellis.

The majority of Florio's works were operettas for Broadway, but in the present instance he apparently aimed somewhat higher and fell somewhat lower than his custom.

"A dark crime was perpetrated," one Philadelphia reviewer began. "A colored person of mature age and saintly character, avuncularly known as Thomas, was cruelly and wantonly tortured and his reputation grossly assailed presumably for the edification of a non-sympathetic public.

"The effect produced on this 'black' Monday was even less satisfying than when the work was done in Italy (and of course in Italian) some fifteen years since. The atmosphere of the theatre was laden with gloom, and on more than one occasion the whole performance suggested the interior of an unpopular church on a very wet Sunday. The music may have produced a feeling of religious fervor with some serious Philadelphians who were present, but as far as others — and we fear the majority — were concerned, they were affected to the verge of open profanity."

Caryl Florio was the pseudonym for Williams James Robjohn. See also Giorza and Ferrari-Trecate.

FLOYD, CARLISLE (1926 -)

The Fugitives

A musical drama in three acts composed in 1951; apparently unproduced.

The Passion of Jonathan Wade — New York (City Center), Oct. 11, 1962

Three acts, with libretto by the composer.

"The work has the virtues of seriousness and sensitiveness, the plot is lively, the characters drawn with a certain sense of delicacy; but both text and music suffer from professional weaknesses.

"All stock characters of the Civil War are present: the noble Union officer, the unregenerate rebel, the stern and upright Southern judge, the carpetbaggers, the Ku Klux Klan, the faithful Negro retainers and, of course, the proud but loving Southern belle." (Paul Henry Lang, in the *New York Herald-Tribune,* Oct. 12, 1962)

Jules Rudel conducted; Norman Triegle, Norman Kelley, Phyllis Curtin, and Theodore Uppmann headed the cast.

The Sojourner and Mollie Sinclair **Raleigh, N. C., Dec. 2, 1963**

An opera in one act with libretto by the composer, commissioned by the Carolina Charter Tercentenary Commission.

"It is a comedy-drama about Scottish settlers of the Carolinas. The Sojourner is a clan chieftain who tries to maintain medieval highland traditions here and Mollie is a forward-looking Scottish lass who wants to leave the old ways behind." (Composer quoted in *The New York Times,* Oct. 13, 1963.) Leading roles were sung by Patricia Neway and Norman Treigle; Jules Rudel conducted. Production was by the opera workshop of East Carolina College.

Susannah **Tallahassee, Fla., Feb. 24, 1955**

Libretto in two acts and ten scenes by the composer. This work became an outstanding critical and popular success when it was performed by the New York City Center Opera Company on Sept. 27, 1956, with Phyllis Curtin singing the title role. It was also given at the Brussels World's Fair in 1958.

The composer derived his book from the Apocryphal Susannah and the Elders, with the locale transferred to the Tennessee mountain valley, a credible setting for the primitive religion with which it deals. The story tells of the Elders' discovery of Susannah bathing in the creek sought by them as a baptismal font. Susannah is branded as evil, and her case is put before the visiting evangelist, Olin Blitch, who exhorts her publicly without success.

She is seduced by Blitch, who then tries to convince the Elders of her innocence. In the end he is destroyed by Susannah's brother and the lonely, embittered woman protects herself from the mob by threat of gunfire. (See also Myron Fink)

Vocal score published by Boosey & Hawkes, 1957.

FOMIN, YEVSTIGNEY (1761 - 1800)

Amerikantsy (The Americans) **St. Petersburg, Feb. 19, 1800**

Comic opera in two acts on an Indian subject with libretto by A. I. Klushin. The vocal score was published in 1893, the full score in 1895. Revived in Moscow 1947.

The story concerns Indians and Spaniards in 16th-century America. There are Don Guzman, his sister Elvira, and, among the Indians, two squaws (Zimara and Zoretta) and their brother Azem. Azem is the Indian Chief. The music, according to Nicolas Slonimsky, is modeled after the Italian manner of the 18th century with arias, duets, and choruses. Guzman and Zimara have a duet (tenor and soprano) "Your Glance is My Paradise," and the Indians have a sun-worshipping prayer, "O Sun, Vanquish these Enemies."

FOSS, LUKAS (1922 -)

The Jumping Frog of Calaveras County — **Bloomington, Ind., May 18, 1950**

Libretto in two scenes by Joan Karsavina based on the story by Mark Twain. Produced at Indiana University, staged by Hans Busch, conducted by Ernst Hoffmann.

"Foss' score manifests considerable rhythmic force and orchestral skill; eclectic in character, the music suggests styles ranging from Wolf-Ferrari to Kurt Weill." (Paul Nettl)

Performed on June 7, 1950 in New York by the After Dinner Opera Company, with the composer at the piano. "While Foss writes more like an American than Weill, a dry cynicism often creeps into the score and removes it in mood from the ambling colloquialism of Mark Twain's story. . . . Nothing is more difficult dramaturgically than to write an effective piece in which the central character never appears." (Cecil Smith)

Vocal score published by Carl Fischer, 1951.

FRANCHETTI, ALBERTO (1860 - 1942)

Cristoforo Colombo — **Genoa, Oct. 6, 1892**

Libretto in three acts by Luigi Illica, with epilogue. Written for the quadricentennial of the discovery of America. Revised and sung at La Scala, Milan, on Dec. 26, 1892 under the direction of Toscanini.

Produced by the Philadelphia-Chicago Grand Opera Company in 1913 with Titta Ruffo and Rosa Raisa. The epilogue was not given.

The music is Meyerbeerian, considered pretentious and without individuality. The plot deals with opposition to Columbus in Spain and on shipboard, adding a subplot involving the murder of an Indian chieftain. The curtain falls on Columbus in chains. Story in Martens.

Vocal score published by Ricordi, 1892.

FREEMAN, HARRY L. (1869 - 1954)

The Flapper

Jazz opera in four acts set in a broker's office and at the Ritz-Carlton Hotel, New York. Not produced.

The Octoroon

Unproduced. Completed in 1904. Libretto in four acts with prologue, based on a story by M. E. Braddon.

The Plantation — **New York, 1930**

Three acts composed 1906-1915. Excerpts were produced with scenery and costumes in 1930 and 1934.

The Tryst New York, May, 1911

Set in a forest in southern Michigan in the days of the pioneers, the story deals with two Indian lovers. Written in 1909.

Valdo Cleveland, 1905

Scene: Mexico. One act with Intermezzo, to a story by the composer. Composed in 1895.

Vendetta New York, Nov. 12, 1923

Scene: Mexico. Three acts.

Voodoo New York, Sept. 10, 1928

Produced at Palm Garden (52nd Street), New York, with scenery and costumes.

Mr. Freeman wrote his own librettos. His works are designated Grand Operas, and were produced by the Freeman Grand Opera Company in Cleveland, Denver, Chicago, and New York variously. (Letter from the composer's son Valdo, Dec. 11, 1957.)

FREER, ELEANOR EVEREST (1864 - 1942)

The Chilkoot Maiden

One act, written about 1927, on an Eskimo subject; set in Skagway, Alaska. Libretto by the composer.

Little Women Chicago, April 2, 1934

Two acts, based on Louisa May Alcott's novel, performed as a monologue in Chicago, 1934.

GABRIELLI, Count NICOLÒ (1814 - 1891)

L'Americano in fiera Naples, 1838

The Indian at the fair.

GAJARDO, REMIGIO ACEVEDO (1863 - 1911)

Caupolicán Chile, 1942

Three acts. Based on primitive defenders of Chile fighting the Spanish invaders. Act I was performed in 1902.

GENÉE, FRANZ RICHARD (1823 - 1895)

Die letzten Mohikaner Vienna, Jan. 4, 1878

Libretto in three acts by F. Zell, this is more properly an operetta. Vocal score published in Hamburg by Cranz, but makes no mention of James Fenimore Cooper, from whose novel the libretto is derived.

GERSHWIN, GEORGE (1898 - 1937)

Porgy and Bess Boston, Sept. 30, 1935

Called a "folk opera," based on the play *Porgy* by Dorothy and Du Bose Heyward; lyrics by Ira Gershwin. Three acts. This most successful of all American operas was done as a Broadway production, opening at the Alvin Theater, on Oct. 10, 1935 with a Negro cast including Todd Duncan, Anne Brown, and John W. Bubbles; Alexander Smallens conducted.

Vocal score published by Gershwin Publishing Co., 1935.

Several times revived; in 1955 toured South America, Europe, and the Soviet Union under sponsorship of the Department of State; made into a motion picture in 1958. *The Muses Are Heard* by Truman Capote (Random House, 1956) is an account of the company's trip to the Soviet Union as the first American theatrical troupe ever to visit there.

GIAMBINI

Il Colombo Parma, 1840

This was a partial performance.

GIANNINI, VITTORIO (1903 -)

The Scarlet Letter Hamburg, June 2, 1938

Four scenes. The composer wrote his own libretto in English; the opera was produced in German as *Das Brandmal.* The distinguished soprano Dusolina Giannini, the composer's sister, sang the role of Hester.

Blennerhasset New York, Nov. 2, 1939

A radio opera, dealing with Aaron Burr's attempt to establish an empire in Louisiana. First performed over the Columbia Broadcasting System.

The Harvest Chicago, Nov. 25, 1961

Libretto by the composer and Karl Flaster. The story is a tragic tale of a well-to-do American farm family in the Southwest at the turn of the century. The principal characters are a blind farmer, his three sons, and the wife of one of the sons. The work was conceived in terms of the pre-Belasco theater.

Four performances, conducted by the composer, were given by the Chicago Lyric Opera. *The Harvest* was the first of four operas commissioned by the Ford Foundation.

Rehearsal Call **New York, Feb. 15, 1962**

Three acts. Libretto by Francis Swann and Robert A. Simon, based on Swann's play *Out of the Frying Pan,* dealing with six aspiring actors (three boys and three girls) in New York City.

"It is a fluffy trifle — a farce, strictly speaking — that as an opera partakes of elements of *La Bohème* by way of *My Sister Eileen.* . . . Mr. Giannini . . . has put everything into this opera, including arch quotes from other composers. . . . There was a good deal of writing in Mr. Giannini's own Puccini-Strauss idiom. . . . *Rehearsal Call* makes no pretense at being big stuff. It is frankly thin, frankly adolescent, frankly derivative. But if nothing else, it is professional in its workmanship. Mr. Giannini knows the human voice and how to write for it. He has composed a three-act opera that should go over big in the workshop circuit (small cast, no chorus, one set, medium-sized orchestra)." (Harold C. Schonberg in *The New York Times,* Feb. 17, 1962)

GIORZA, PAOLO (1832 - 1914)

La Capanna dello zio Tom **Milan, Nov. 10, 1853**

Based, of course, on Harriet Beecher Stowe's *Uncle Tom's Cabin;* originally titled *I Bianchi ed i negri,* the whites and the blacks, produced at La Scala, Milan, as a ballet.

See also Ferrari-Trecate and Florio.

GLEASON, FREDERICK GRANT (1848 - 1903)

Montezuma

The composer wrote his own libretto in three acts. Apparently unproduced.

GOLDBECK, ROBERT (1839 - 1908)

Those of Goldbeck's works to which reference is found — *Newport, Saratoga, The Soldier's Return* — are musical comedies. Many of his manuscripts were lost in the Chicago fire of 1871.

GOMES, ANTONIO CARLOS (1836 - 1896)

Il Guarany **Milan (La Scala), Mar 19, 1870**

"The most successful Brazilian opera, and the only one by a South American composer which has been in the active repertoire of opera houses the world over." (Slonimsky) Written to an Italian libretto by A. Scalvini (revised by C. d'Ormeville), after a Brazilian novel by José de Alencar. The central figure is an Indian of the Guarany tribe, and the work contains Amazon themes.

Story in Martens. Vocal score published by Hutchings & Romer, 188-.

This work was produced in Rio de Janeiro on Dec. 2, 1870, and in New York on Nov. 3, 1884.

The composer's *Colombo* is an oratorio.

GRAUN, KARL H. (1704 - 1759)

Montezuma — **Berlin, Jan. 6, 1755**

Libretto (in French) in three acts by King Frederick II. Score published as Vol. XV of *Denkmäler deutscher Tonkunst,* 1904.

GRÉTRY, ANDRÉ E. M. (1741 - 1813)

Le Huron — **Paris, Aug. 20, 1768**

Libretto for this comic opera in two acts by J. F. Marmontel, based on a story by Voltaire entitled *L'Ingénu; ou, le Huron.* An analysis of the plot is given in Martin Cooper: *Opéra Comique* (Chanticleer Press, 1949).

Vocal score published by Beraux, 1768.

GRUENBERG, LOUIS (1884 -)

The Emperor Jones — **New York (Metropolitan), Jan. 7, 1933**

Prologue and two acts; text by K. de Jaffa, based on the play by Eugene O'Neill, with scene on an island in the West Indies. The composer was given free rein by the author to adapt the play as he saw fit; the music contains one Negro spiritual: "Its-a-me, O Lord, its-a-me, standin' in the need o' prayer."

"Nowhere is his music impediment to the progress of the drama. Nowhere does it cloud the speech or the action by the play prescribed. But nowhere does it much enhance or animate it either. The life and power of *The Emperor Jones* as opera still springs from the play and performance." (H. T. Parker, in *The Boston Evening Transcript*)

Lawrence Tibbett scored one of his greatest successes in the role originally associated with Charles Gilpin.

Kaiser Jones, as it was known in Germany, was well received at the Berlin Opera under the direction of Erich Kleiber, 1933.

Vocal score published with English and German text by Cos Cob Press and Universal-Edition.

GUARNIERI, CAMARGO (1907 -)

Malazarte

Libretto in one act by Andrade, based on a Brazilian legend; unproduced.

HAAN, WILLEM DE (1849 - 1930)

Die Inkasöhne **Darmstadt, 1895**

Subject: the Incas of Peru.

HADLEY, HENRY K. (1871 - 1937)

Azora, Daughter of Montezuma **Chicago (Auditorium), Dec. 26, 1917**

Libretto in three acts by David Stevens.

The libretto was not praised. "Of Mr. Hadley's music words of greater commendation must be expressed. There is a great deal that is fine in the score. Nor should there be omitted a word of admiration for Mr. Hadley's orchestration." (Felix Borowski) Anne Fitziu, Forrest Lamont, Arthur Middleton, and Cyrena Van Gordon were in the cast. There were many vacant seats in the Auditorium. Three performances. The same cast sang the work in New York at the Lexington Theater, on January 26, 1918, where it was greeted by a larger audience; the composer conducted.

Vocal score published by G. Schirmer, 1917.

HALÉVY, JACQUES (1799 - 1862)

Jaguarita l'Indienne **Paris, May 14, 1855**

Libretto in three acts by J. H. Vernoy de St.-Georges and A. de Leuven, drawn remotely from James Fenimore Cooper's *The Spy*. Pawnee Indians are portrayed, and Creoles. The work was sung in New Orleans on Jan. 18, 1859.

Vocal and full scores published by Heinz, 1885.

L'Éclair **Paris, Dec. 16, 1835**

Comic opera in one act, taking place on a "plantation" near Boston in 1797. Story in Martens. The work was produced in New York in 1866. Full and vocal scores published by Schlesinger, 1836.

HALL, WILLIAM JOHN (1867 - 1931)

Louisiana **St. Louis, 1904**

An operatic extravaganza for the St. Louis Exposition.

HANSON, HOWARD (1896 -)

Merry Mount — **New York (Metropolitan), Feb. 10, 1934**

Libretto in three acts by Richard L. Stokes, after *The May-Pole Lovers of Merry Mount,* a story by Nathaniel Hawthorne. The scene is a Puritan settlement near Quincy, Massachusetts, in 1625. Story in John Tasker Howard: *Our American Music.*

Sung in concert form at Ann Arbor, Michigan, on May 20, 1933, with John Charles Thomas, Leonore Corona, Frederick Jagel, and Rose Bampton, the composer conducting. The Metropolitan Opera cast featured Lawrence Tibbett, Göta Ljungberg, Gladys Swarthout, and Edward Johnson, with Tullio Serafin conducting. There were fifty curtain calls.

"*Merry Mount* should make its way into the public heart." (Lawrence Gilman)

The choruses were considered most successful; music for the Rev. Wrestling Bradford was "not savage, not frenetic enough."

The work stands as "a passionate protest against the moral hypocrisy, tainted with cruelties and repressions, which persisted in the American psychology from the day of Plymouth Rock to the day of the Volstead Act." (Gilman)

See also David Stanley Smith's work on the same subject. An operetta *Puritan Days* by Earl Marble and Richard Stahl, produced in 1884, was warmly commended; it follows the same story.

Vocal score published by Harms, 1933.

HANSON, WILLIAM F. (1887 -)

The Sun Dance — **Vernal, Utah, Feb. 20, 1913**

Five acts. Based on a Sioux Indian ceremony. Libretto by the composer. The work was subsequently performed in other cities of Utah, and in New York in 1938.

Tam-Man-Nacup — **Provo, Utah, May 3, 1928**

Based on a Uintah Indian ceremony. The composer conducted the first performance; the work was also produced at the University of Utah, Salt Lake City, with the Los Angeles Philharmonic.

HARLING, W. FRANKE (1887 - 1958)

A Light from St. Agnes — **Chicago, Dec. 26, 1925**

Lyric tragedy in one act with libretto by Minnie Maddern Fiske; set in Louisiana. Story in Martens. The score makes incidental use of jazz with saxophones, banjos, and snare drums. One performance.

Rosa Raisa sang the role of Toinette. So great was the success of the Chicago première that 200 persons pursued, hugged and kissed the composer in a near-riot. Coming home to Boston, he was greeted without fanfare at South Station by his father, sexton of the Old South Church, his mother, and his brother. The Chicago Civic Opera Company did not present the work on its subsequent Boston visit.

"The record of a small community in old Louisiana tells of the life and works of a certain Agnes who used her great wealth in doing good. On the summit of a hill not far from her home there stood a convent, and to this retreat she returned in the last years of her short life. She built a chapel named for her patron saint and from this chapel she was buried." (Martens)

The work was sung with success in Paris, June 1929, with Eleanor Painter, Rafaelo Diaz, and Howard Preston in leading roles. It was acclaimed as the first jazz opera to be heard in Europe.

Vocal score published by Huntzinger, 1925.

Deep River **Lancaster, Pa., Sept. 18, 1926**

A "native opera with jazz"; libretto by Lawrence Stallings, author of *What Price Glory?* Scene: New Orleans, 1830.

The opera was taken to Philadelphia for a two-week run at the Shubert Theater, followed by two weeks in New York. Jules Bledsoe and Rose McClendon headed a large cast, the composer conducting. Story in Martens.

HATTON, JOHN LIPTROTT (1809 - 1886)

Pizarro **London, 1856**

Incidental music for the play by Sheridan.

HAUFRECHT, HERBERT (1909 -)

Boney Quillen **Chichester, N. Y., 1961**

Libretto in three scenes by the composer. A thirty-minute pantomime opera set in the Catskills. Vocal score published by Broude Bros., 1953.

Boney Quillen was an eccentric who lived at the turn of the century, a Civil War veteran, lumberman, prankster, jokester, maker of verses and songs. This work was commissioned by Camp Woodland, Phoenicia, New York, for the 1951 Folk Festival of the Catskills, held in Chichester.

HAWKINS, MICAH (1777 -)

The Saw Mill; or, A Yankee Trick

A ballad opera in two acts, performed on an unknown date, at the Chatham Theater, New York, and mentioned as "the first genuine American opera."

HERBERT, VICTOR (1859 - 1924)

Natoma — Philadelphia, Feb. 25, 1911

Libretto in three acts by Joseph D. Redding, a San Francisco lawyer. The setting is a mission at Santa Barbara, California, and the Island of Santa Cruz, in 1820. Story in Martens.

Sung in New York on Feb. 28, 1911, and afterwards in Baltimore, Chicago, Los Angles, and San Francisco. The world première by the Philadelphia-Chicago Grand Opera Company was conducted by Cleofonte Campanini, with Mary Garden and John McCormack in the leading roles. Six performances.

To many it seemed that the millennium had come. Arthur Nevin's *Twilight* followed soon at the Metropolitan; his *Poia* had been sung the previous year at the Berlin Opera. Converse's *The Pipe of Desire* had been heard at the Metropolitan, and his *The Sacrifice* was scheduled for the Boston Opera Company. Five thousand persons attended the Philadelphia première of *Natoma,* and the following day's press conveyed a statement by the prima donna that the long-drawn-out kiss which had so intrigued the audience was not a real kiss at all. Tickets sold for thirty dollars, the audience applauded wildly, spectators greeted Herbert with shouts, cheers, and laurel wreaths from over the footlights, Miss Garden skipped on and off stage, and there was a reception in the foyer. Meanwhile — and meanly — the critics were letting Herbert down as politely as they could in critical honesty.

The New York Times reported that the work was not convincing as drama expressed by music, and that the music was better than the libretto. Lyrics were of the type referred to by Voltaire as based on the theory that what is too foolish to say may be properly sung. Herbert utilized Indian melodies and leading motives, although not exactly in the Wagnerian manner.

Vocal score published by G. Schirmer, 1911.

HEWITT, JAMES (1770 - 1827)

Columbus

Composed in 1799.

Pizarro; or, The Spaniards in Peru

Incidental music to Sheridan's play, composed in 1800.

Tammany; or, The Indian Chief — New York, Mar. 3, 1794

Libretto in three acts by Mrs. Anne Julia Hatton. The music is lost, and the lyrics only are extant.

Sung three times in New York, twice in Philadelphia, and once in Boston. The text is notable for "impossible flights of poetic imagination," and was referred to as "that wretched thing." Mrs. Hatton was a sister of the famous actress Mrs. Siddons, and the wife of an instrument maker in New York.

Tammany, a noble Indian chieftain, loves dusky Manana. One of Columbus's ignoble followers, Ferdinand, carries her off. When "her shrill cries through the dark woods resound," Tammany comes to the rescue without success. Tammany and his beloved squaw are burned in their wigwam by the Spaniards while a chorus of Indian priests sings a dirge.

For fuller discussion of this work, significant because it is the first Indian opera — or at least, so proclaimed, see Sonneck's account in *Early Opera in America.* Dunlap, a vengeful Federalist, dubbed it "literally a mélange of bombast."

One aria, "Death Song of the Indian Chief," was published.

The Patriot; or, Liberty Asserted **1794**

A ballad opera.

HOOK, JAMES (1746 - 1827)

The Fair Peruvian **London, Mar. 8, 1786**

Comic opera adapted from Marmontel's *L'Amitié à l'épreuve.*

HOPKINSON, FRANCIS (1737 - 1791)

The Temple of Minerva **Philadelphia, Dec. 11, 1781**

The composer referred to this work as both an "Oratorial entertainment" and a "Musical Entertainment," but Sonneck holds that it was actually an operatic entertainment in two scenes. He reminds us that it belongs in the class with those mythological-allegorical-political operas fashionable in the courts of Europe wherein the monarch was glorified as head over all. Sonneck writes: "If Andrew Barton's *The Disappointment; or, The Force of Credulity* (1767) was the first comic ballad opera produced by a native American, that is to say, a comedy interspersed with songs, Francis Hopkinson's *The Temple of Minerva* would have to be considered as our first attempt at 'grand opera.' With this term I mean an operatic entertainment in which everything is sung, nothing spoken, for, though the lines given to Minerva, the Genius of France, the Genius of America, and the High Priest of Minerva are not inscribed as 'airs,' there can be little doubt that they were sung either as airs or recitatives."

Sonneck is careful to point out that in Colonial times "oratorial" was derived from oratory, and not from oratorio, and that, as a rule, a musical entertainment meant an "opera."

The work was in two scenes, the first in the Temple of Minerva; in the second "The doors of the Sanctuary are open." The libretto is given from the only surviving copy in *Francis Hopkinson and James Lyon,* printed for Oscar G. Sonneck by H. L. McQueen in 1903:

> The Temple of Minerva. An Oratorial Entertainment performed in Nov. 1781 by a company of Gentlemen and Ladies in the Hotel of the Minister of France in Presence of his Excellency General Washington and his Lady. [The correct date was Dec. 11, 1781]

The score is lost.

Hopkinson, at no time a professional musician, was a distinguished amateur of music, an active servant of his country during the Revolution, and a signer of the Declaration of Independence.

HOUSELEY, HENRY (1852 - 1925)

Ponce de Leon

Three acts with libretto by Randolph Hartley.

Native Silver

Operetta in three acts, produced in Denver, c. 1891.

HUGO, JOHN ADAM (1873 - 1945)

The Sun God

Libretto by Rev. Bartlett B. James. Subject: Pizarro and the Incas of Peru. Apparently unproduced.

The Temple Dancer, a one-act opera by Hugo, was produced at the Metropolitan in 1919; other works were heard in Germany.

HUMMEL, FERDINAND (1855 - 1928)

Assarpai — Gotha, 1898

Libretto in three acts by Dora Dunker, based on a story by Wildenbruch on the subject of the Incas in Peru. Story in Martens. A work in the Italian veristic manner.

Vocal score published by Simrock, 1898.

HYDE, F. S.

An opera on the subject of King Philip's War in New England, 1675, is mentioned by Hipsher, but no further information is available.

JONES, ABBIE GERRISH (1863 - 1929)

Priscilla

Romantic opera in four acts, with libretto by the composer. Composed in 1885-1887 but not performed. This is probably the first opera by an American woman. See Mary Carr Moore. Set in New England before the Revolution, on a theme of witchcraft.

The Aztec Princess

Probably not completed.

JONES, DANIEL

The Knife **London (Sadler's Wells), Dec. 2, 1963**

Opera in two acts, commissioned by the Welsh Committee of the Arts Council, with libretto by the composer. One performance.

A Negro is saved from lynching in a Southern mining town of the United States when a conscience-stricken white man confesses to raping and murdering a white girl for which crime the Negro is held. Time: 1866.

"If you don't like the piece, you will say that it is old-fashioned. But . . . you cannot accuse Mr. Jones of clumsiness or incompetence. Bravely eschewing stylization he has given us a plot with lively situations, and big, singable leading parts, and his full orchestra and chorus play and sing in a swelling romantic style. . . . The performance, conducted by David Lloyd-Jones, was a remarkably successful effort . . . with a strong, eloquent characterization of the Negro by Frank Olegare." (Edmund Tracy, in *The London Observer,* Dec. 9, 1963)

JONGEN, LÉON (1885 -)

Thomas l'Agnelet, Gentilhomme de Fortune **Brussels, Feb. 14, 1924**

Libretto in four acts by Claude Farrière after his novel of buccaneering. The scene is a ship sailing for the Spanish Main.

JOPLIN, SCOTT (1869 - 1917)

A Guest of Honor

The manuscript of this "ragtime opera" has disappeared; it was copyrighted but not published; performed, in concert, in St. Louis at an undetermined date.

Treemonisha

Preface to the published score gives September 1884 as the time. There are three acts taking place on Morning, Afternoon, and Evening of the same day when "Tremonisha, being eighteen years old, now starts upon her career as a teacher and leader." "The Scene of the Opera is laid on a plantation somewhere in the State of Arkansas, Northeast of the Town of Texarkana and three or four miles from the Red River. The Plantation being surrounded by a dense forest." These two quotations are respectiveely the last and first sentences of the Preface; in the intervening two pages Joplin sketches the story of Negroes of his plantation between 1866 and 1884, when the action takes place. Ned and his wife, Monisha, having no child of their own, find a two-day-old baby under a tree.

The cast includes three sopranos, three tenors, one high baritone, and four basses, plus a chorus. There are ten numbers in the first act, eight in the second, and nine in the third. There is an overture beginning with a ragged theme which Joplin identifies as "the principal strain in the Opera and represents the happiness of the people when they feel free from the conjurers and their spells of superstition." One number has a cast of eight bears who sing "Oo-ar!" and dance a waltz.

The work was orchestrated, but performed in concert form with piano in Harlem, New York, on an unidentified date. A deposit copy of the score, giving no publisher's name, is in the Library of Congress.

JORDAN, JULES (1850 - 1927)

Mr. Jordan's works, including *Rip van Winkle,* were light operas often sung by the famous Bostonians. He served as his own librettist. *Rip* was produced at the Providence Opera House on May 25, 1897, composer conducting.

KASTLE, LEONARD (1929 -)

Deseret **New York, Jan. 1, 1961**

The libretto by Anne Howard Bailey calls for six characters and a normal orchestra. Subject: the search by Brigham Young and the Mormons for their Promised Land, called Deseret, which is the present State of Utah. This work was announced for production in an off-Broadway theater in 1959; financial and artistic problems proved too great. It was produced on television by the NBC Opera Company in New York.

Mr. Kastle is a graduate of the Curtis Institute of Music. A fifteen-minute opera in one act entitled *The Swing* was produced by the National Broadcasting Company on television in 1956 and at Carl Fischer Hall, New York.

An item in *The New York Times* of Feb. 2, 1960 discussed the possibility of producing *Deseret* in Moscow as part of a projected exchange of new American and Soviet works. The Union of Composers of the Soviet Union, receiving the score through the Soviet Embassy, stated; "The music drama of the opera is developed in a colorful manner. The expressive melody and songlike quality are precise and psychologically sharp and acute in the characterization."

See also works on this subject by Johann Brandl and Dudley Buck.

KAUER, FERDINAND (1751 - 1831)

Inkle und Yariko **New York, Aug. 8, 1798**

One act, based on Coleman, written in collaboration with Josef Alois Gleich. See Samuel Arnold for another work of the same title.

KAUFMANN, WALTER (1907 -)

The Scarlet Letter **Bloomington, Indiana, May 6, 1961**

An opera in three acts based on the novel by Hawthorne with libretto by the composer. Scene: Salem, Massachusetts, in the 17th century. This work, produced by the School of Music, Indiana University, received several performances and was revived in 1962; it was also sung in Indianapolis on Jan. 30, 1962.

The composer is a member of the faculty. This is his fifth opera, the first written in the United States.

KELLEY, EDGAR STILLMAN (1857 - 1944)

Puritania; or, The Earl and the Maid of Salem **Boston, June 9, 1892**

Comic opera in two acts with libretto by C. M. S. MacLellan.

Act I takes place in Salem, Massachusetts. The maid is accused of witchcraft, but the charge shows "that her weird influence is nothing more than the magnetic power of innocence and lovely girlhood." As she is about to be convicted, His Majesty's ship from England is seen in harbor being an official investigator who falls in love with the maid and takes her back to England for legal trial and, eventually, legal marriage (which may or may not be the same thing).

Of the music the press wrote: "Offenbach could not be more persuasive — Arthur Sullivan might well be envious. Respectful consideration is due to *Puritania* for its freedom from vocal waltzes, topical songs, and Amazon marches. The music and costumes outweigh the text."

Vocal score published by John Church, 1895.

KELLY, MICHAEL (1762 - 1826)

Pizarro **London, 1799**

Incidental music for Sheridan's play, composed and selected by Kelly from Gluck, Sacchini, and others.

"Expectation was on tip-toe; and strange as it may appear, *Pizarro* was advertised, and every box in the house taken, before the fourth act of the play was begun; nor had I one single word of the poetry for which I was to compose the music." A lengthy account of the Sheridan-Kelly collaboration on this work is given in Kelly's *Reminiscences* (1826), Vol. II.

In *Letters from Greenroom Ghosts* (Viking Press, 1935), John Mason Brown has included a chapter entitled "Richard Brinsley Sheridan to Noël Coward," from which the following is an excerpt:

"Taking intentional advantage of the patriotic feelings the Napoleonic wars had created in England . . . I made from Kotzebue's *The Spaniards in Peru, or, The Death of Rolla,* that adaptation entitled *Pizarro* which filled the coffers of Drury Lane as it was acted there by Kemble, Mrs. Siddons and Mrs. Jordan, and which was crammed with such resolute fustian that it long remained an actor's favourite in English-speaking countries. But the real Sheridan who was willing to sign his name to the bombast of *Pizarro* was not the Sheridan who had written either *The School for Scandal* or *The Rivals.* That other Sheridan had already been dead for two decades, and in his place had come a humourless dramatist who was willing to indulge in all the excesses of false tragedy which the true Sheridan would have hated and which he had once ridiculed to perfection in *The Critic.*"

Jan Dussek and Thomas Linley also wrote incidental music for Sheridan's play.

The Indian London, 1800

KERRISON, DAVENPORT

The Last of the Aztecs

Grand opera with libretto by the composer, completed in 1914. Scene: Mexico City, 1519 and 1520.

KING, MATTHEW PETER (1773 - 1823)

The Americans London, 1811

This is the romance of Little Chittibaw, the Indian:

Yanky, tanky, chaninky, tinky,
I'm a pretty squaw,
I'm in love with Chittibaw.

Some of the music was by John Braham (Abraham); the famous song "The Death of Nelson" is from this work.

"Braham came forward once to sing one of his most famous and familiar songs, and for his life could not recall the first line of it — he told his mishap to the audience, and they screamed it at him in a chorus of a thousand voices." (Oliver Wendell Holmes in *The Professor at the Breakfast Table.*)

KNOWLTON, E. BRUCE (1875 - 1941)

Montana Portland, Oregon, 1933

Opera in two acts with a mining background.

Wakuta Portland, Oregon, Oct. 14, 1928

An Indian subject with contemporary treatment in four acts, set in the great Pendleton Round Up and Indian reservations in Oregon and Idaho. Produced by the American Opera Company, composer conducting.

The Woodsman Portland, Oregon, April 4, 1929

Three acts set in Pacific Northwest with a background of the lumber industry. Produced by the Bruce Knowlton Opera Company, Inc.

Mr. Knowlton was one of the most active Western musicians, but has not yet found his place in musical dictionaries. His early training was in Illinois and Wisconsin, but he also studied in Berlin, Dresden, London, and Paris. He founded the Toledo (Ohio) Conservatory of Music and was President of the St. Paul

(Minnesota) Musical Academy. After 1921 he lived in Portland, where he was active as conductor and teacher. It is said that his scores were written in an idiom no longer fashionable even in his own day, but they were nonetheless skillfully composed. He was his own librettist, and his scores are in the Oregon State Library, Salem. (Letter, Jan. 26, 1958)

KORN, CLARA ANNA (1866 - 1940)

Their Last War

An opera in manuscript.

KRENEK, ERNST (1900 -)

Jonny spielt auf — Leipzig, Feb. 10, 1927

The libretto in two parts (eleven scenes) is by the composer. The work is American in its use of jazz, and in the circumstance that at the conclusion Jonny stands at the North Pole proclaiming: "The New World comes across the sea in radiance and inherits ancient Europe by means of the dance."

The work was produced in Paris in 1928, and at the Metropolitan in New York (in German) on Jan. 19, 1929.

Jonny fared badly in Vienna and even worse in Budapest, owing to political unrest. Hundreds of policemen cleared space near the opera house and plain-clothes men were inside. Anti-Jewish demonstrations were prevalent at the time, but Mr. Krenek was a "German-Bohemian," and a Christian. "Bruno Walter did not conduct, from which we may gather that he did not agree with its artistic convictions." *(The Christian Science Monitor)*

"The Metropolitan clientele which refused to accept in calmness the Strauss-Wilde version of the Biblical lady who had a preference for severed heads, cannot be imagined stomaching the incidents wherein the Negro Jonny makes expressive love to the white serving maid to her obvious delight, and bestows his insistent but unwelcome attentions on the prima donna. . . . Krenek s opera is as alert as Jonny's jazz, and as provocative of pleasure and discussion." *(The Boston Evening Transcript)*

"Note that in New York Jonny becomes, not a Negro, but a black-face comedian. Mr. Bohnen's face was black, but his neck remained unmistakably white. . . . There is jazz in (the music), but very early jazz which will probably cause customers of musical comedy to clamor at the box-office for their money back." *(The Christian Science Monitor)*

Vocal score published by Universal-Edition, 1926.

KREUTZ, ARTHUR (1906 -)

The University Greys — University of Mississippi, Mar. 15, 1954

An opera in two acts (nine scenes) with libretto by Zoe Lund Schiller

(Kreutz) based on a book of the same name by Maud Morrow Brown. The scene is Mississippi during the War Between the States. Commissioned by the University in 1953 and performed by a cast of students. Revived on May 1, 1961 to commemorate the centennial of the 11th Mississippi Regiment's departure from the campus.

The story deals with a boy who enlisted in the Greys and went off to war, returning to the campus to die, with his childhood sweetheart to whom he is married in Oxford during his first leave, with events surrounding these episodes. The work, scored for full orchestra and requiring chorus and ballet, takes about two hours for performance. Vocal score published by Ricordi.

The University Greys constituted a regiment drawn from men at the University, not one of whom returned to the campus. Characters and episodes in the story, however, are fictional.

Kreutz is a winner of the Prix de Rome and two Guggenheim Fellowships in composition; a symphony was played by the New York Philharmonic in 1945 under Artur Rodzinski. Kreutz is associate professor of violin and composition. His ballad opera *Acres of Sky* was produced at Columbia University, N. Y., on May 7, 1952, and his one-act folk opera *Sourwood Mountain* had its première at the University of Mississippi on Jan. 8, 1958.

A critic wrote that the score was "fearsomely modern" with "astringent atonalities," having some "moments reminiscent of Menotti and a few others of Stravinsky," an analysis probably describing local musical receptivities rather than an idiom beyond its time.

LAMBORD, BENJAMIN (1879 - 1915)

Woodstock

Unproduced; only two acts completed.

LEONI, FRANCO (1864 - 1949)

L'Oracolo — London, June 28, 1905

The one-act libretto by C. Zanoni is based on *The Cat and the Cherub* by Fernald; the scene is Chinatown, San Francisco, before the Fire. Story in Martens. Chim-Fen, keeper of an opium den, steals a child and hides it in his cellar. In the Metropolitan production (Feb. 4, 1915), Antonio Scotti made this opera a vehicle for his remarkable talents.

"In spite of Leoni's music, the grisly drama is still powerful. . . . Poor Leoni did his best, but he is not the man to write drama on a tragic text." (Philip Hale, *The Boston Herald*)

Leoni was a successful composer, but his works were in a style earlier than that current in his time, especially in view of the Verdian ethic.

Vocal score published by Chappell & Co., 1905.

Rip van Winkle — London, Sept. 4, 1897

Libretto by William Ackerman-Boosey. Gretchen is a patient wife, rather than a shrew as usually portrayed. Rip is lured to the Catskill mountains by a "skirt dancer" who waltzes as he falls asleep. When he comes back to his friends, it is in the midst of an election campaign for first United States Senator with Knickerbocker and Derrick as opposing candidates. Seeing his wife after a twenty year absence, Rip asks: "Katrina, my dear, how are you?"

Rip was sung with an Irish brogue in London, but that was not the reason for its failure. It has never been sung in America.

Vocal score published by Ricordi, 1897.

LEROUX, XAVIER (1863 - 1919)

Évangeline **Brussels, Dec. 18, 1895**

Libretto in four acts by Grammont, Hartmann, and Alexandre, with scene in Louisiana. Story in Martens.

The travels of Evangeline in search of Gabriel, which require one-third of Longfellow's poem, are compressed into one short Third Act. Act IV takes place in a hospital in Pennsylvania where Evangeline has become a sister of charity, as the poet envisioned the setting, and the characters retain their original names.

This work seems never to have been produced in the United States.

Vocal score published by Choudens, 1895.

LIEURANCE, THURLOW (1878 - 1963)

Drama of the Yellowstone

Written about 1919 but apparently not produced.

LINLEY, THOMAS (1733 - 1795)

Robinson Crusoe; or, Harlequin Friday **London, Jan. 29, 1781**

This was actually a pantomime, based on Sheridan's play after Defoe. Pantaloon, Harlequin, and Columbine hold their usual place after the first act.

Linley was Sheridan's father-in-law.

Pizarro

Incidental music to Sheridan's play.

LISTOV, KONSTANTIN (1900 -)

Cuba's Daughter **Voronezh, June 25, 1962**

Opera by a Soviet composer on the life of a Cuban girl guerrilla fighter, Angela Alonso, still active in the Castro regime at the time of the production.

LLANOS Y BERETA, A.

Colombo — **Naples, 1892**

LOBO, ELIAS ALVARES (1834 - 1901)

A Noite de São João (St. John's Eve) — **Rio de Janeiro, 1860**

Two acts. The first Brazilian opera in the Portuguese language. Based on a story by José Alencar.

LOCKE, MATTHEW (1630 - 1677)

The History of Sir Francis Drake — **London, 1658**

Incidental music to a play of Sir William Davenant.

LOCKWOOD, NORMAND (1906 -)

The Scarecrow — **New York, May 19, 1945**

Two acts. Based on witchcraft in Salem, Massachusetts. Produced at Columbia University.

Early Dawn — **Denver, Colorado, Aug. 7, 1961**

An opera in three acts with libretto by Russell Porter, based on an original play of the same name. Scene: Illinois on the day of the outbreak of the Civil War. It is a theme of a house divided as brothers are torn between love and patriotism, when public feeling is so impassioned that it allows no time for considered judgment as to which cause is preferable.

"The orchestra is large . . . but above it is [the composer's] songfulness, full-hearted folk-song, that catches the ear and tugs at the feelings. The musical idiom, like the story it supports, is as home-spun as calico, and just as tough.

"The opera should take its place on the lengthening list of American works that borrow their settings from the sweep of the American land and dream." (*The Christian Science Monitor*, Sept. 8, 1961)

The work was staged by Edwin Levy and conducted by Thomas Sherman. Normand Lockwood is composer-in-residence at the University of Denver, and this production was part of its centennial commemoration.

LORTZING, GUSTAV ALBERT (1801 - 1851)

Die Schatzkammer des Inka

Libretto by Robert Blum, *The Inca's Treasure Chest.* This unproduced work is not in the composer's usual comic vein, but is a romantic opera taking place in Peru; it was written in 1836. Only one number is extant, a march.

LUENING, OTTO (1900 -)

Evangeline **New York, May 5, 1948**

Libretto in four acts by the composer. Written in 1932. Produced at the Columbia University Festival, N. Y., with the composer conducting. Excerpts were performed in Chicago on Dec. 29, 1932.

MAEDER, JAMES GASPARD

Ponce de Leon

The composer lived in the United States; this work was written about 1861.

MAJO, GIOVANNI (1732 - 1770)

Montezuma **Venice, 1765**

Libretto by V. A. Cigna-Santi.

MANNING, EDWARD B. (1874 - 1948)

Rip van Winkle **New York, Feb. 12, 1932**

Libretto by the composer.

MARCORA, C. (1839? - 1869)

Cristoforo Colombo **Bahia, Brazil, 1869**

MARETZEK, MAX (1821 - 1897)

Sleepy Hollow; or, The Headless Horseman **New York, Sept. 25, 1879**

Libretto in three acts by Charles Gaylor.

"Maretzek leads us back at least twenty-five years; his style of writing has nothing in common with the modern manner of operatic style. It takes us back to the time of Bellini, Donizetti, and the young Verdi. Maretzek has remained free of a foreign influence; his style is Italian from beginning to end.

"New York with its cosmopolitan character, with its mixed population, can digest stronger food, and is ripe to listen to operas of a more elaborate character. But we must not forget that Maretzek has written for the whole country. . . . It is no use to present an opera on an American subject to a farmer out West, and give him high-toned music, which this poor man will not understand at all.

"But we found honest work, honest labor, in it, and we think this opera will do more good in the West than *Lohengrin* on the one side, or *Pinafore* on the other.

"The music is light and pleasing, there is nothing vulgar in it, and for this reason alone it deserves honorable mention. The melodies are well conceived and the vocal part is sufficiently well prepared. The instrumentation is interesting; even the xylophone is taken into consideration and used on several occasions with great effect. The first act is best, for it contains the principal musical work and is suited best to the operatic stage. Among others we may mention an ensemble of great value; this piece is well written and must everywhere make an effect." (J. S. Dwight, Oct. 4, 1879)

The above would appear to display Dwight's usual supercilious attitude toward the West and all that it contained. It is true that the Bostonian air was rarefied beyond endurance in this very period, but Dwight knew full well that Maretzek's career at this point was made successful by touring. Travelling opera companies such as his comprise a saga as yet untold in our time. They included a host of excellent singers and instrumentalists, many with fine European reputations, playing in "opry" houses and converted railroad stations to audiences ranging from newly rich gold miners to newly poor Indians in blankets.

MARKOE, PETER

The Reconciliation; or, The Triumph of Nature

Comic opera in two acts founded on Gessner's *Erastus*, published, but not produced, in Philadelphia, 1790.

MARQUÉS Y GARCÍA, PEDRO MIGUEL (1843 - 1918)

La Manja Alférez — Madrid, 1875

"The Nun Ensign." Scene: Peru and Chile.

MARYON, EDWARD (1867 - 1954)

The Smelting Pot

An unproduced work in three acts with libretto by the composer; set in New York's East Side. The score is dedicated to the memory of Walt Whitman.

The Werewolf

Libretto in four acts by the composer; dedicated to Edgar Allan Poe. Set in "a northern State in the Union," the home of John Quincy. Unproduced.

Maryon also wrote "an American Ballet Pantomime" entitled *Rip van Winkle*. His full scores, in the Music Department, Boston Public Library, show him to have been an accomplished composer of the post-Wagnerian school.

MASSENET, JULES (1842 - 1912)

It may be noted here that this composer's *Manon* does not venture beyond France. See works by Auber and Puccini.

MATTAUSCH, ALBERT (1883 -)

Die Jassabraut **Magdeburg, 1922**

Libretto by Bethge, based on Kleist's *Die Verlobung in Santo Domingo,* taking place near Port-au-Prince about 1803. Story in Martens.

MATTHEWS, JOHN SEBASTIAN (1870 - 1934)

Narragansett Pier

Mathews was a composer of serious works, but this was probably a comic operetta. It remains in manuscript.

MAURI, JOSE (1856 - 1937)

La Esclava **Havana, 1921**

Libretto by Thomas Julia. The tragic tale of a presumably white heroine, during the late period of Spanish rule, who discovers that she is of slave blood. This is a folk opera.

MÉHUL, ÉTIENNE (1763 - 1817)

Alonzo et Cora **Paris, Feb. 15, 1791**

Libretto in four acts by Valadier, founded on Marmontel's novel *Les Incas.*

MELA, VINCENZO

Cristoforo Colombo **Verona, 1857**

MENDELSSOHN-BARTHOLDY, FELIX (1809 - 1847)

Die beiden Neffen; oder, Der Onkel aus Boston **Feb. 7, 1824**

Properly an operetta; three acts, with libretto by Dr. Caspar. Privately performed on the composer's 15th birthday.

Zelter, a friend, wrote the youthful composer: "My dear boy, from this day forward you are no longer an apprentice but a journeyman in the brotherhood of musicians. I proclaim your emancipation in the name of Mozart, Haydn, and old father Bach." A synopsis of the work, with copious musical examples, may be found in G. Schünemann's article on the juvenile operas of Mendelssohn in *Zeitschrift für Musikwissenschaft,* 1925, p. 50ff. In this his fourth opera, the composer began to show mature skill; he now sought longer melodic lines, larger form, the brighter ensemble. The next opera, *Die Hochzeit des Camacho,* was an adult work. The score is unpublished. Prof. Eric Werner has seen it and states that "the operetta is well-conceived, but both textually and musically of a rather philistine quality."

A young man, destined to become a famous singer, Eduard Devrient, acted in all these youthful works, attended by his fiancée Theresa, to whom he was married soon after this period. Devrient wrote: "This work, in comparison with his first operas, gave manifest tokens of progress in command of melody and vocal part writing. Theresa and I assisted at a series of amusing rehearsals of this work and at the two performances of the music, the dialogue being read between the pieces."

The chief characters are Fanny, Lisette, Theodore, and Carl, and the scene is unidentified but could be anywhere. The Boston uncle does not appear until the third act.

MENOTTI, GIAN-CARLO (1911 -)

Le dernier Sauvage **Paris (Opéra-Comique), Oct. 21, 1963**

Opéra-bouffe in three acts, libretto by the composer. Commissioned by the Opéra-Comique in an effort to bring new life to the repertory.

The plot concerns Kitty (coloratura), a student at Vassar and her millionaire father, Scattergood, of Chicago on a visit to India. Kitty's desire to capture an Abominable Snowman as subject for an anthropology paper leads to hilarious exploits in India and in Chicago, many of them probably comprehensible only to Americans. Menotti's music brings in "new hindsights on Rossini," and makes occasional open use of Puccini, Genêt reports in *The New Yorker* (Jan. 2, 1963).

The American première at the Metropolitan Opera on Jan. 23, 1964 was sung in English *(The Last Savage).*

The Old Maid and the Thief **New York, April 22, 1939**

Libretto in fourteen scenes by the composer, suggested by the town of West Chester, Pennsylvania. Commissioned and first performed on the radio by the National Broadcasting Company; the first stage production was by the Philadelphia Opera Company on Feb. 11, 1941.

Vocal score published by Ricordi, 1943.

The Saint of Bleecker Street **New York, Dec. 27, 1954**

Libretto in three acts (five scenes) by the composer, set among the Italian community in the lower East Side of New York. Commissioned by Lincoln Kirstein for the New York City Center Opera Company but found to be too expensive for production there; produced at the Broadway Theater by Chandler Cowles. Also produced at La Scala, May 1955, and Basel, December 1955.

"Italian verismo opera with a dash of psychology added to it." (Olin Downes) The New York cast featured David Poleri, Virginia Copeland, and Gloria Lane; Thomas Schippers conducted. 84 performances.

"Whistles of disapproval in La Scala, a cool reception in Vienna, a tremendous success in Basel." *(The Christian Science Monitor)*

Vocal score published by G. Schirmer, 1955.

MEYEROWITZ, JAN (1913 -)

The Barrier **New York, Jan. 18, 1950**

Libretto in two acts by Langston Hughes, based on his *Mulatto* and *Father and Son.* Subject: race relations in Georgia. Produced at Columbia University. Score reproduced from holograph in New York Public Library.

Eastward in Eden **Detroit, Nov., 1951**

Libretto in five scenes by Dorothy Gardner, based on her play of the same name on the life of Emily Dickinson in Amherst, Massachusetts. Produced at Wayne University.

"If some of Meyerowitz' music were considered apart from the opera it would seem inventive, and not without interest in its turgid, thickly-orchestrated way. But in conjunction with its action on the stage it only caused wonder that a composer would react musically the way he did to the dramatic situations. The vocal line seemed awkward, without justification for the musical, dramatic, or prosodic reasons." *(Musical America,* June 1954*)*

MIGNONE, FRANCISCO (1897 -)

O Contratador dos diamantes **Rio de Janeiro, Sept. 20, 1924**

An episode during the 18th-century exploration of Brazilian diamond mines.

MILHAUD, DARIUS (1892 -)

Christophe Colomb **Berlin, May 5, 1930**

Libretto in two acts (27 scenes) by Paul Claudel; produced in a German version by R. S. Hoffmann.

Vocal score published by Universal-Edition, 1930.

The composer also wrote music for the Jean Louis Barrault play, utilizing an orchestra of only thirteen instruments. This was an entirely different score. In the opera, America is shown only in a brief bit of land on which Columbus places the flag with the cross, a filmed scene. There are as many speaking parts as singing roles, the action is carried on by a narrator, and a chorus lines either side of the stage into the audience.

Maximilien Paris, Jan. 4, 1932

Libretto in three acts (nine scenes) by R. S. Hoffmann, translated into French by A. Lunel, based on Franz Werfel's play *Juarez und Maximilian.* Story approved by the Belgian, Austrian, and Mexican legations in consideration of living persons who were associated with the events portrayed.

"The composer has created in disregard of all tradition, and has given us a work which is violent, apocalyptic, which gives off venomous fumes like the pot of the three witches in *Macbeth." (Le Temps)*

Vocal score published by Universal-Edition, 1931.

Bolivar Paris (Opéra), May 12, 1950

Libretto in three acts (ten scenes) by Jules Superveille and Madeleine Milhaud. Composed in 1943.

MINSHULL, JOHN

Rural Felicity New York, 1801

New Year's Morning New York, 1831

No further information.

MONCADA, BERNARDO

Teresa

Opera in three acts based on an episode of the Cuban revolution against Spain in 1895. Destroyed by the composer.

MOORE, DOUGLAS (1893 -)

The Ballad of Baby Doe Central City, Colorado, July 7, 1957

Libretto in three acts by John Latouche, based on the life of Horace Austin Tabor (1830-1899), mining magnate and politician who served as United States Senator for six weeks in 1881. Tabor's wealth vanished when the country adopted the gold standard, and the price of silver dropped.

This work, performed by the New York City Center on April 3, 1958, has been one of its most successful ventures. Sixteen performances were given in Colorado. Scenes were telecast in February 1957. Won the New York Music Critics Award in 1958.

"An operatic Western." "The Girl of the Silver West." "Apart from *Porgy and Bess* and *The Mother of Us All,* no single American work has mirrored so clearly the life of an era and a people." *(New York Herald Tribune)* William Jennings Bryan and Chester A. Arthur are introduced as characters. The original cast featured Walter Cassel and Martha Lipton.

Vocal score published by Chappell, 1958.

The Devil and Daniel Webster **New York, May 18, 1939**

A folk opera in one act with libretto by Stephen Vincent Benét, set in New Hampshire during the 1840's. The most frequently performed opera on an American subject by a native composer.

Vocal score published by Boosey & Hawkes, 1943.

Giants in the Earth **Columbia University, New York, March 28, 1951**

Libretto in three acts by Arnold Sundgaard after a novel by Rolvaag. Set in a Norwegian settlement in Dakotah territory about 1870. Won the Pulitzer Prize.

"There is very little sustained power in the libretto; the action moves with marked unevenness, and at times with lapses of dramatic interest. There are continuous evidences of outstanding musical quality and dramatic movement in the score."

The Headless Horseman; or, A Legend of Sleepy Hollow **Bronxville, N. Y., 1937**

Libretto in one act by Stephen Vincent Benét, based on Irving's story, with a twist satirizing progressive schools and their teachers.

Vocal score published by E. C. Schirmer Music Co., 1937.

White Wings **Hartford, Feb. 2, 1949**

A chamber opera in three acts based on the play by Philip Barry.

The Wings of the Dove **New York, Oct. 12, 1961**

An opera in six scenes, not divided into acts, based on the novel of the same name by Henry James. Scenes are in London, Venice, and in the National Gallery (London).

Performed as the first work sponsored by the Ford Foundation on its schedule of regional opera enterprises at the New York City Center. Directed by Julius Rudel, the cast included Regina Sarfaty, Martha Lipton, Dorothy Coulter, Norman Kelly.

"Can you really call *The Wings of the Dove* an American opera? Certainly it is about Americans — not the kind known to Daniel Webster in Vermont or to Baby Doe in Colorado, but surely known to the time and place of Henry James — specifically, such a time as 1900, and such places as London and Venice." (Irving Kolodin: *Saturday Review,* Oct. 28, 1961)

MOORE, HOMER (1863 - 192-)

The Puritans **St. Louis, 1902**

Deals with Salem witch hunting.

Columbus; or, The New World **St. Louis, 1903**

The story of the discovery, with Columbus' return to Spain. There are Spanish and Indian scenes designed to give color. Not intended as "music drama" but a guiding theme is employed. The choruses were considered the most successful part of the work. It was sung with the composer in the leading role, assisted by 32 pupils, and by Charles Kunkel at the piano. Mr. Moore travelled widely, and had a long career as singer, teacher, and conductor; he was particularly interested in the music of Richard Wagner. He wrote his own librettos.

The Pilgrims

These three works comprised an "American Trilogy," the first two sung in concert, the third apparently unproduced and possibly uncompleted.

MOORE, MARY CARR (1873 - 1957)

The Flaming Arrow **San Francisco, March 27, 1922**

An "Indian Intermezzo" in one act. The composer conducted the first performance.

Narcissa (originally entitled *The Cost of Empire*) **Seattle, April 22, 1912**

Text by Sarah Pratt Carr, the composer's mother. Scene: the Pacific Northwest. The first grand opera to be written, staged, and directed by an American woman. Story in Martens. This work memorializes the career of Dr. Marcus Whitman, a missionary and patriot in Oregon, during the early 1830's. Dr. Whitman met his death at the hands of the Indians.

Revived during California's Diamond Jubilee Celebration (San Francisco, Sept. 7, 1925).

Vocal score published by Witmark, 1912.

Los Rubios **Los Angeles, Sept. 10, 1931**

Three acts; libretto by Neeta Marquis. Based on the early history of Los Angeles (c. 1857); includes Indian and Spanish melodies.

Mrs. Moore conducted more than forty performances of her works for the musical stage.

MORALES, JULIO MELESIO (1838 - 1908)

Cristoforo Colombo a San Domingo **Mexico City, Oct. 12, 1892**

Libretto in one act by Enrico Golisciani.

MORLACCHI, FRANCESCO (1784 - 1841)

Colombo **Genoa, June 21, 1828**

Text by Felice Romani. Two acts. See Carnicer's opera to the same libretto.

MOROSS, JEROME (1913 -)

Gentlemen, Be Seated! **New York (City Center), Oct. 10, 1963**

"One act opera with popular songs and dialogues" — the composer. Libretto by Edward Eager. There are twenty-two set numbers following the sequence of the Civil War. There is soft-shoe dancing but no ballet. While the style and form of the minstrel show of the period are followed, end men are Negroes and there are Negroes in the chorus.

Produced with a grant from the Ford Foundation.

"After the promising opening, most of the minstrel elements are dropped, and what "Gentlemen, Be Seated!" turns out to be is nothing more or less than a slick musical comedy. . . . Indeed, there is something flippant about the book and its score. It deals with great issues and great events. Bull Run, Shiloh, Appomattox, Andersonville; those shivering, terrifying names. The Emancipation Proclamation, Abraham Lincoln, Mathew Brady, 'Stonewall' Jackson. Even within the confines of a musical comedy there should be respect for what they represent. . . . Musically the score is a pastiche. It uses elements of spirituals, Civil War songs, ragtime, jazz, sentimental ballads — but most of it is in a language stemming straight out of Richard Rodgers." *(The New York Times,* Oct. 12, 1963)

MÜLLER, ADOLF (Sr.) (1801 - 1886)

Domi, der amerikanische Affe **Vienna, Jan. 28, 1831**

MÜLLER, WENZEL (1767 - 1835)

Die Prinzessin von Kakambo **Vienna, Nov. 19, 1814**

A Peruvian subject based on Kotzebue. Two acts; text by J. Perinet.

Vitzilipututzli **Vienna, Feb. 14, 1817**

Singspiel in three acts on a Mexican subject, with libretto by Franz Rosenau.

MYSLIVEČEK, JOSEF (1737 - 1781)

Motezuma **Florence, Jan., 1771**

Libretto in three acts (the same used by Zingarelli) by V. A. Cigna-Santi.

NEVIN, ARTHUR (1871 - 1943)

A Daughter of the Forest **Chicago, Jan. 5, 1918**

Libretto in one act by Randolph Hartley, originally called *Twilight*. Scene: Western Pennsylvania during the Civil War; this is not an Indian opera. Sung by Forrest Lamont and Frances Peralta, Campanini conducting. The work is entirely lacking in dramatic motivation. One performance.

Vocal score published by John Church, 1917.

Arthur Nevin is not to be confused with his brother, Ethelbert, composer of *Narcissus* and *The Rosary*.

Poia **Berlin, April 23, 1910**

Libretto (in English) by Randolph Hartley; German translation by E. von Huhn. Three acts. Subject: Blackfoot Indians of Montana. Story in Martens. First performed in concert form in Pittsburgh, Jan. 15, 1906, where the press considered it "destined to take its place among the greatest of the world's classics." *(Pittsburgh Dispatch)*

In Berlin the work was victim to strong feelings against an American work usurping the stage of a national opera. "No onslaught in all past history of savage musical and dramatic criticism in Berlin has ever excelled in downright abuse and violence the treatment accorded Arthur Nevin's American grand opera *Poia*." *(Boston Herald)* There was also much discussion as to how the production came about, and why this work was selected. Charges of payment to the Berlin opera, or of personal influence, were denied by the composer, who attributed the work's failure to the temper of the times.

Vocal score published by Fürstner, 1909.

OFFENBACH, JACQUES (1819 - 1880)

La Périchole **Paris, Oct. 6, 1868**

Libretto in two acts by H. Meilhac and Ludovic Halévy, on the usual Peruvian subject; expanded to three acts (Paris, April 25, 1874).

This work was widely performed by an able French troupe throughout the eastern part of the United States in 1869, and it remained a favorite work in America until the end of the century, particularly as a vehicle for Lillian Russell in 1895. The Metropolitan Opera revived the work in 1957 in a new version with English text by Maurice Valency.

Vocal score published by Brandus & Dufour, 1868.

Robinson Crusoé **Paris, Nov. 23, 1867**

Libretto in three acts by E. Cormon and H. Crémieux. The story has slight resemblance to the Defoe tale, and Crusoe has no lack of male or female companionship. A young woman, Susanna, is cast ashore with him. Crusoe is a tenor. Act I takes place in Bristol, England, in the house of Sir William Crusoe, Acts II and III in South America, at the mouth of the Oronoco River.

Vocal score published by Brandus & Dufour, 1867.

La Créole Paris, Nov. 3, 1875

Libretto in three acts by A. Millaud, H. Meilhac, and Ludovic Halévy. The scene is Guadalupe.

An English version, entitled *The Commodore,* was given in London and New York in 1886.

Vocal score published by Choudens, 1875.

ORTEGA, ANICETO (1823 - 1875)

Guatimotzin

The first Mexican opera on a native subject. One act. Composed about 1867. The cast includes Guatemoc, the last Aztec Emperor, and Cortez.

ORTÍZ DE ZÁRATE, ELIODORO (1865 - 1953)

La Fiorista di Lugano Santiago, Chile, Nov. 1, 1895

"The first opera by a Chilean composer performed in Chile." (Letter from the Pan American Union, 1958)

Lautaro 1902

Based on the story of an Araucanian hero celebrated by Erçilla.

OTTOBONI, CARDINAL PIETRO (1667 - 1740)

Il Colombo; ossia, l'India scoperta Rome, Dec. 28, 1690

Three acts. Cardinal Ottoboni, nephew of Pope Alexander VIII, wrote the libretto; it is not known whether he also composed the music. This is the earliest Columbus opera; the score is lost.

PAISIELLO, GIOVANNI (1740 - 1816)

Le Gare generose Naples, 1786

Libretto in two acts by Giuseppe Palomba. Performed in many countries under varying titles.

Mr. Dull, a Boston merchant, frees two white girls who have been made slaves.

Libretto published by P. F. Fauche, 1795.

PASMORE, HENRY B. (1857 - 1944)

Amor y oro

Libretto by James Gaily, on a story from California history. Pasmore's *Miles Standish* is an overture.

PATTERSON, FRANKLIN P. (1871 -)

A Little Girl at Play

One act. A tragedy of the slums. Cast comprises three characters; there is no chorus.

Mountain Blood

Three acts, after Hergesheimer; composed in 1915.

PATTON, WILLARD (1853 - 1924)

Pocahontas — **Minneapolis, Jan. 4, 1911**

Sung in concert form.

PELISSIER, VICTOR

Columbus; or, The Discovery of America — **Baltimore, 1783**

The Launch; or, Huzza for the Constitution — **Boston, Sept. 20, 1797**

A pasticcio, with music selected, and "new Orchestra parts by Pelissier." Hodgkinson played the lead, and the work concluded with a striking scenic representation of launching the new frigate *Constitution,* with views of Charlestown, Massachusetts.

The Fourth of July; or, Temple of American Independence
New York, July 4, 1799

The scenery included views of the Battery, Harbor, and Broadway.

These three works were ballad operas or "allegorical musical dramas."

PEREIRA, ELPIDIO (1872 -)

Calabar

Libretto by Eugenio and Edmundo Adenis, set in Brazil during the Dutch wars. Unproduced.

PETRELLA, ERRICO (1813 - 1877)

I Pirati spagnuoli — **Naples, May 13, 1838**

PHELPS, ELLSWORTH C. (1827 - 1913)

The Last of the Mohicans

Mentioned by Hipsher; no further information.

PICCINI, NICCOLÒ (1728 - 1800)

L'Americano ingentilito — **Rome, Feb. 20, 1772**

A two-act intermezzo. "The ennobled Indian."

I Napolitani in America — **Naples, 1768**

PIGNANI, ENRICO (1836 - 1894)

Cristoforo Colombo — **Genoa, 1883**

In collaboration with Penco.

PLANQUETTE, JEAN-ROBERT (1848 - 1903)

Rip van Winkle: A Romance of Sleepy Hollow — **London, Oct. 14, 1882**

Libretto by Dion Boucicault, changed by Meilhac and Gille; English version by Farnie. The composer's most successful work, apart from *Les Cloches de Corneville;* ran for 328 nights in London, and is now occasionally revived on European stages.

In this version Rip's wife is a charming girl, rather than a shrew; Rip goes to the mountains to escape English soldiers and to seek buried treasure. He returns to find his daughter grown, and there is a charming bit in the score when he identifies himself by singing a childhood song which he taught the girl. The part of the daughter in Act III is sung by the same person who portrayed his wife in Act I, inasmuch as they resemble each other. Act III is also made lively by the introduction of an election campaign with speeches, and the demonstration of new methods of balloting.

The work was sung in New York (Oct. 28, 1882, in English), and in Mexico City (June 7, 1885, in Spanish).

Vocal score published by Stoddart & Co., 1882.

Surcouf — **Paris, Oct. 6, 1887**

Opéra comique in three acts with text by Chivot and Duru. For the English production H. B. Farnie changed the libretto to follow outlines of J. F. Cooper's *The Pilot* and the title was *Paul Jones, an American Pirate*. This work ran for 330 nights in Paris, and for an entire season (1890) in London, with the part of Paul Jones sung by a woman!

Vocal score published by Bathlot, 1887, and in Boston by White-Smith, 1888.

PORTOGALLO, MARCOS (1762 - 1830)

Fernando nel Messico **Venice, Jan. 16, 1798**

Libretto in three acts by F. Tarducci. Written for Elizabeth Billington; produced in London (in Italian) on March 31, 1803. The composer's most successful work.

Portogallo emigrated to Brazil in 1811, remaining there until his death. A partial autograph of the score is in the Bibl. da Ajuda, Lisbon.

PRATT, SILAS GAMALIEL (1846 - 1916)

The Triumph of Columbus **New York, Oct. 12, 1892**

Libretto by the composer in five acts. Heard in concert form only.

Pratt's opera *Ollanta,* to his own libretto, was never performed.

PUCCINI, GIACOMO (1858 - 1924)

La Fanciulla del West **New York (Metropolitan), Dec. 10, 1910**

Three acts. Libretto by C. Zangarini and G. Civinini, based on David Belasco's play *The Girl of the Golden West*. It is California matter in the Italian manner, the story suggesting Bret Harte, Shaw's *Blanco Posnet,* Frank Norris, or Richard Watson Tully, not to mention the countless horse-operas on which a large segment of the film public dotes. The whole thing is a study in rascality, and the rascality of the Californians is in exact proportion to their sentimentality. Will Minnie marry the Sheriff? No; she and the outlaw will start life anew somewhere else.

"The emptiest thing yet put on the market by the celebrated Italian composer." (Olin Downes)

Emmy Destinn, Enrico Caruso, and Pasquale Amato sang the leading roles, with Toscanini conducting. Oddly, the score is dedicated to Queen Alexandra.

"The first German production . . . was greeted by respectful attention and a fair amount of applause, but there was a notable lack of anything approaching enthusiasm. The types represented in the opera are as incomprehensible to Germans as men from Mars would be." *(New York Times)*

Vocal score published by Ricordi, 1910, and by Boosey & Co., 1910.

Revived at the Metropolitan in 1929 with Maria Jeritza, Giovanni Martinelli, and Lawrence Tibbett. Filmed in 1938 with Nelson Eddy, Jeanette MacDonald, and Walter Pidgeon in the leading roles. Sung in Chicago, Dec. 27, 1910,

Boston, Jan. 17, 1911. Revived on opening night at the Metropolitan Oct. 23, 1961 with cast including Leontyne Price, Richard Tucker, Anselmo Colanzi.

Madama Butterfly — **Milan (La Scala), Feb. 17, 1904**

Libretto by L. Illica and G. Giacosa in two acts (later in three) founded on a story by John L. Long as dramatized by David Belasco. The action does not take place on American soil, but has one American character, Lt. Pinkerton.

Produced in Buenos Aires on July 2, 1904, Washington, D. C. on Oct. 15, 1906 (in English), and in New York on Nov. 12, 1906 (in English). At the first Metropolitan performance (Feb. 11, 1907, in Italian), the leading parts were sung by Geraldine Farrar, Caruso, and Antonio Scotti, with Arturo Vigna conducting; Puccini was present.

The opera failed at La Scala after one performance. "The audience howled with derision." "The audience simply went wild with enthusiasm" in New York, but the work "seemed cruel and repulsive" in Boston.

Vocal score published by Ricordi, 1904.

Manon Lescaut — **Turin, Feb. 1, 1893**

Libretto in four acts by M. Praga, D. Oliva, L. Illica, and the composer, based on the novel by the Abbé Prévost. Act IV takes place in New Orleans.

Produced in Philadelphia, Aug. 29, 1894, and New York, May 27, 1898.

Vocal score published by Ricordi, 1915.

PUERNER, CHARLES

The Trumpeter of New Amsterdam

Puerner's works were written for the Broadway theater.

PURCELL, HENRY (1658 - 1695)

The Indian Queen — **London, 1695**

Music for Dryden's play (1664); Queen Zempoalla is arrayed in Aztec feathers. The ballad "I attempt from love's sickness to fly" is from this work. Elaborate machinery of the original performance included battles, sacrifices, spirits singing in the air, and the god of dreams rising through a trap door.

RABITI, SANGIORGIO

Il Colombo — **Parma, 1840**

RALPH, JAMES (- 1762)

The Disappointment; or, The Force of Credulity

American comic opera in two acts with verses by Andrew Barton, a name which may have been assumed. Rehearsed in Philadelphia but not produced. The tune "Yankee Doodle" was used.

Libretto published in New York, 1767. A second edition was published in Philadelphia, 1796, by Francis Shallur, with changes and expansion into three acts.

"Until James Ralph is positively proven not to have been born in America, *The Disappointment* will have to be considered *the first American opera."* (Sonneck) Story in Sonneck's *Miscellaneous Studies in the History of American Music,* p. 25ff.

On April 20, 1767, "a new Comic Opera, called the *Disappointment* . . . was announced, with date of performance, but subsequent events make plain that its basic idea — the search for hidden treasures of the pirate Captain Blackbeard — would hold up to public ridicule well-known Philadelphians who were seriously engaged on such a project." The libretto survives in several collections, and a page is reproduced in *Early Operas in America.*

Hum, Parchment, Quadrant, and Rattletrap, making a Philadelphia tavern their headquarters, invent a map to show where a fictional Captain Blackbeard hid his treasure. Their dupes, Washball and Raccoon, at length find a pirate's chest filled with stones, as the practical jokers run from the stage.

REEVE, WILLIAM (1757 - 1815)

The Purse; or, American Tars — **Charleston, S. C., Feb. 8, 1797**

This was an Americanized version of Reeve's *The Purse; or, the Benevolent Tar,* which had been introduced two years before with a libretto by Cross.

Produced in New York, Jan. 29, 1798.

REINAGLE, ALEXANDER (1756 - 1809)

Columbus; or, A World Discovered — **Philadelphia, Oct. 20, 1797**

Pizarro; or, The Spaniards in Peru — **Philadelphia, 1800**

Incidental music for the play written in collaboration with Raynor Taylor.

We may well mourn the loss of these scores, for Alexander Reinagle was a musician of taste. His career, both in this country and abroad, is not yet fully known, and it will be chronicled only with difficulty; but he had as strong an influence (for the good) on the music of his time as did any other musician in America. Some of Reinagle's music was composed before he came from England, but it is probable that the above scores were written for the immediate occasions.

REPUBLICANO, ANTONIO DE ASSIO (1897 -)

Amasonas

Prologue and three acts on an Inca subject.

REZNIČEK, EMIL VON (1860 - 1945)

Satuala **Leipzig, Dec. 4, 1927**

Opera in three acts with libretto by Rolf Lauckner. Scene: Hawaii at the time of the American landing in 1893.

A beautiful fair-skinned native girl bewitches the American Captain for a sufficiently long time to enable the Hawaiian irreconcilables to attack the landing forces. With fine operatic irony, however, the lady falls in love with the earnest captain. After he commits suicide to the strains of The Star-Spangled Banner (off-stage) she stabs herself to death. The score is one of romantic inflation with bristling syncopation in secundal harmonies; there is a hula-hula ballet, but generally the score is securely post-Wagnerian. (Story and description supplied by Nicolas Slonimsky.)

Vocal score published by Universal-Edition, 1928.

RICCI, LUIGI (1805 - 1859)

Il Colombo **Parma, June 27, 1829**

L'eroina del Messico **Rome, Feb. 9, 1830**

Ricci wrote thirty operas, one of which *(Crispino e la comare)* was performed at the Metropolitan Opera in 1919.

RICE, EDWARD E.

Evangeline

Opera buffa based on the poem by Longfellow, with libretto by J. Cheever Goodwin. Published in 1877.

ROBYN, ALFRED GEORGE (1860 - 1935)

Robyn's works were all comic operas or musical comedies and were produced in New York by Henry Savage.

ROGATIS, PASCUAL DE (1881 -)

Huemac **Buenos Aires, July 28, 1916**

Lyric drama of a Chibchamecan priest who, in 600 A.D., led five tribes from Huehuetlapallan to the valley of Mexico. Italian libretto in one act by E. Montagne.

La Novia del hereje — **Buenos Aires, June 13, 1935**

Four acts, based on the colonial epoch in Argentina.

ROLLA, ALESSANDRO (1757 - 1841)

Pizarro; o, la conquista del Peru — **Milan, 1807**

Rolla was a teacher of Paganini.

ROOT, GEORGE F. (1820 - 1895)

The Haymakers — **c. 1859**

Operatic cantata in two acts for amateurs; contains directions for use of a platform if regulation stage is not available. Extensive use of recitatives. Program of first performance in Upton, *Musical Memories* (Chicago, C. McClurg, 1908). Vocal score published by Mason Brothers.

ROSSINI, GIOACCHINO A. (1792 - 1868)

La Cambiale di matrimonio — **Venice, Nov. 3, 1810**

Libretto of this *farsa comica* in one act by Gaetano Rossi. Rossini's first performed opera, written in a very few days, when the composer was but sixteen years old. The overture had been composed previously. The orchestration was considered too heavy by singers who demanded that he follow traditional patterns. The story concerns a North American colonist, Mr. Slook, who arrives in 18th-century London to purchase a bride. According to Francis Toye, the work contains two attractive airs, a first class trio, and a very fine duel scene. "It may be doubted whether previous opera, Mozart's *Entführung,* and Cimarosa's *Matrimonio Segreto* not excepted, had ever before been characterized by such sparkle, such a wholly irresponsible sense of fun."

Vocal score published by Schonenberger, 184-.

This work was presented in America by the Salzburg Opera Guild, 1937, in what was probably its first professional production here.

Sung in concert by the Little Orchestra Society, New York, March 1, 1961.

SÁNCHEZ DE FUENTES, EDUARDO (1874 - 1944)

Doreya — **Havana, Feb. 7, 1918**

Libretto by Hilarión Cabrisas, suggested by the discovery, in 1915, of the first pre-Columbian Indian burial grounds on the island of Cuba. Story in Martens.

The composer was also a distinguished author of books on Indian music, military bands, and on the construction of the pianoforte.

SCHOENEFELD, HENRY (1857 - 1936)

Atala; or, The Love of Two Savages

Indian opera in three acts, with a libretto by Bernard McConville adapted from the novel by Chateaubriand. Scene: Florida. Not produced.

SCHROEDER, HERMANN (1843 - 1909)

Pizarro; oder, Die Eroberung von Peru

SCHUMAN, WILLIAM (1910 -)

The Mighty Casey Hartford, May 4, 1953

Libretto in three scenes by Jeremy Gury, set in "Mudville, U.S.A."

Based on Ernest L. Thayer's poem, *Casey at the Bat,* recitation of which provided De Wolf Hopper with an income for many years. Oddly, only Ring Lardner among the literary men and women seems to have glorified our national sport.

"One has the uneasy feeling, indeed, that the music to *The Mighty Casey* could be transposed intact to, say, the New York Telephone Directory, or Kant's *Critique of Pure Reason,* and serve very much the same purpose." *(New York Times)* "The spirit of *The Mighty Casey* is parody; but as parody it does not entirely succeed. The humor is too superficial, on the whole, to deserve the title of comedy." *(The Christian Science Monitor)*

The Composer's Showcase (Charles Schwartz, Director) sponsored a "First Public Performance" at the Museum of Modern Art, New York, on May 11, 1961.

SESSIONS, ROGER (1896 -)

Montezuma West Berlin Opera, April, 1964

An opera in three acts and eleven scenes on text by Antonio Borghese, dealing with the last Aztec Emperor.

SHIELD, WILLIAM (1748 - 1829)

The Poor Soldier London, Nov. 4, 1783

This work was a favorite with General Washington; it deals with the adventures of a gallant continental, and the locale was changed to America for its New York production, Dec. 2, 1785, and many successive performances. Under its original title *The Shamrock,* it was produced in London on April 7, 1783.

SKILTON, CHARLES SANFORD (1868 - 1941)

Bluefeather

Libretto in one act by Lillian W. Spencer, based on Pueblo Indians. In manuscript.

Kalopin

Libretto in three acts by Virginia Armstead Nelson. An Indian opera; composed in 1927, but unproduced. Set in New Madrid about 1811, the cast includes Chickasaw and Choctaw Indians; a system of leitmotives is employed. New Madrid is fictionally located on the banks of the Mississippi in Tennessee.

The Sun Bride **New York, April 17, 1930**

An Indian opera in one act; first performance on the radio (National Broadcasting Company).

SMITH, DAVID STANLEY (1877 - 1949)

Merry Mount

Libretto by Lee Wilson Dodd in three acts. Unproduced.

"Mr. Lee W. Dodd and I wrote it, I think in 1911, more for the enjoyment of the work than out of any particular ambition to succeed in opera. . . . I do think that *Merry-Mount* has qualities. . . . I think that there is more warmth and color than in most of my music. . . . To be sure, the managers of the Opera (Metropolitan) seem to find it difficult to understand this work (because they don't know enough about American history) . . . Alfred Herz . . . was extremely interested in the work and made vain efforts to have it performed." (Letter to Artur Bodansky, Nov. 12, 1919.)

Full score and vocal score are in the library of the Yale University School of Music.

SOBOLEWSKI, EDUARD DE (1808 - 1872)

Mohega; or, The Flower of the Forest **Milwaukee, Oct. 11, 1859**

Libretto (in German) by the composer.

"A musical drama by Eduard Sobolewski, late conductor and director of the royal opera at Königsberg, Prussia, and of the opera at Bremen, has brought out a musical drama in Milwaukee of North America. Mr. Sobolewski is a pupil of the great Carl von Weber. We are told that there is not a man in America capable of passing judgment on the effort of Sobolewski, and that until the score reaches the *Leipzig Neue Zeitschrift für Musik,* the criticism of America must remain suspended . . . *Mohega* will stand or fall upon its inherent worth regardless of the dictum of those intensely scientific and critical journals of operatic Germany.

"*Mohega* is entitled by the libretto 'an Episode of the American Revolution.' The first act is located in the valley of Wyoming, and the audience are treated to the noisy parts of the massacre which there took place. The whole of this act is full of startling effect — rapid action — and quick transitions from scene to scene. . . . Not a moment serene, not a moment swelling, but in those transparent 'sheets of melody' that we may rise, the expression whereon one has time to catch the reflection of elaborated passion or highly wrought sentiment. Its own hurry and activity destroys the images we look for. And yet, if the music lacks depth, its activity more than compensates in this act, in which there is little sentiment to express, and all the scenes partake of the didactic rather than of the emotional character.

"The second act affords us *sweet* music, brilliant but never powerful. We begin to feel pity for Ellen, who between Butler and Pequod sustains alternating persecution, which culminates in the savage tying her to a tree and, after lighting the fire which is to consume her, amuses himself in fancying she is a target, at which our pity leaves us and a slight sense of the ridiculous takes its place. The introduction of the *Star-Spangled Banner* — aside from its being an anacronism — in this connection has the semblance of burlesque, especially as Pulaski sings a verse of it in English, and dwells determinedly on unemphatic words. We question the taste which puts this comparatively recent song into the mouths of Revolutionary heroes. It bears the appearance of claptrap. Pequod, having exhausted his arrows in tormenting Ellen, suddenly and, I think unaccountably, falls asleep during the very loud lullaby of Ellen.

"The third act draws the catastrophe in true 'Bowery style.' Butler fires his pistol at Pulaski and wounds Ellen instead; Pulaski is himself mortally wounded immediately. Pulaski shoots Butler, and Mohega dies because her true love dies. Having thus disposed of the chief characters, naught remains but to wave the American flag over them, which is done and the chorus sings us the last verse of the *Star-Spangled Banner*.

"It cannot but strike the careful auditor who has perused the libretto that there is great discrepancy between this flimsy plot and the instrumentation. The latter is thoroughly brilliant, the former tame and hackneyed. . . . The drama passes before us like a well-ordered spectacle *accompanied* with instrumental music of the greatest excellence. The plot is vigorous but heartless.

"In conclusion, we submit that Mr. Sobolewski's opera has but given us the feeblest taste of his musical ability, and when he learns to estimate the musical taste of the Western country a little more, his next work will be a greater success than this." *(Milwaukee Weekly Sentinel,* Oct. 17, 1859)

The entire history of Eduard de Sobolewski urgently requires full investigation by scholarly dissertation. May a capable graduate student soon embark on such a project! Schumann spoke well of his *Komala* (1848), which Liszt produced at Weimer in 1858.

SOUTHARD, LUCIEN H. (1827 - 1881)

The Scarlet Letter — **Boston, Aug. 1855**

Libretto in three acts by F. H. Underwood. The score is lost.

Omano — **(Concert) Boston, 1858**

An opera on Indian life with libretto in Italian. Manuscript in the Boston Public Library.

Three scenes were performed at a miscellaneous concert, featuring Mrs. J. H. Long, Boston's ablest soprano. Mrs. Long had a distinguished career, and was the first voice teacher of Geraldine Farrar.

"January 9th: sang for Mr. L. H. Southard at Chickering's Hall, Masonic Temple, in selections from his Opera *Omano,* Mr. C. H. Adams tenor, Mr. Powers, basso, Miss Susie Whitehouse, alto, took parts and an audience splendid in quality and quantity. The music decidedly original and sparkling with the wonderful genius of the author. It made a decided impression and many were heard to say 'it is equal to anything in the Italian School of opera' and many expressed the hope that we might see and hear the entire opera on the boards of our splendid Boston Theater here. Mr. B. J. Lang and Southard were 'orchestra.' " (unpublished diary of Mrs. J. H. Long in the Boston Public Library.)

"It is not too much to say that it was the most decided and legitimate success that has yet come within our knowledge in the history of American efforts at musical composition in the larger forms. Mr. Southard has evidently studied Gluck, Mozart, Cherubini, and Spontini, not to say the recitatives of Handel and Mendelssohn not in vain. Some of the orchestral harmonies and modulations were mystical and almost Freischütz-like, and others bright and rapturous as the theme required." (John Sullivan Dwight, in *Dwight's Journal of Music.*)

SPELMAN, TIMOTHY MATHER (1891 -)

La Magnifica

Libretto in one act by Leolyn Louise Everett (the composer's wife); set in South America about 1800. Composed in 1920. Full score published by J. & W. Chester, c. 1924.

The Courtship of Miles Standish

Composed in 1943 to a libretto by Mrs. Spelman, based on Longfellow's poem.

SPONTINI, GASPARO (1774 - 1851)

Fernand Cortez; ou, La Conquête du Mexique — Paris, Nov. 28, 1809

Libretto in three acts by V. J. Étienne de Jouy and J. A. Esménard, after the tragedy by Alexis Piron. The story deals with the fate of Spanish prisoners caught in the city of Mexico as Cortez beleaguered it. A work favored by Napoleon I who attended the first performance.

Produced at the Metropolitan, New York, on Jan. 6, 1888 (in German), but considered a work of antiquarian interest only. Popular in its day, however, it ranks below *La Juive.*

"A great deal of recitative, often in the style of Gluck, there is; some magnificent choruses, a wealth of graceful ballet music, and a Trio in act one that is poetic and pathetic. When the time of its writing is considered, *Cortez* is after all a very meritorious opera. It was produced here no doubt because it furnishes opportunities for great spectacular effect." (*New York Herald,* Jan. 7, 1888)

Vocal score published by Érard, 1817; pianoforte score by Hofmeister, 183-.

STEWART, HUMPHREY JOHN (1856 - 1932)

Montezuma **San Francisco, 1903**

Music for a play, with text by Louis A. Robertson. Stewart's works are musical comedies or operettas: *The Conspirators, Gold, John of Nepomuk.*

STILL, WILLIAM GRANT (1895 -)

A Bayou Legend

Two acts, composed 1940.

A Southern Interlude

Libretto in two acts by Verna Arvey, the composer's wife; written in 1942; unproduced.

Blue Steel

Three acts, composed about 1935, but not produced.

Troubled Island **New York (City Center), Mar. 31, 1949**

Libretto in three acts by Langston Hughes, set in Haiti, 1791. Libretto published by Leeds Music Corp., 1949.

STORACE, STEPHEN (1763 - 1796)

The Cherokee **London, Dec. 20, 1794**

Text by J. Cobb, in three acts. This is the story of a young Indian who imagines himself going to London, where all in Bond Street will admire his fashion. "With tomahawks and rings and hatchets hung to strings, every belle will seem a squaw."

A "patter song" in Act I reads:

Oh, what a fight it was to see, what a din, what a glorious rattle!
And I so snugly perched up in a tree, had a bird's eye view of the battle!
There were Chockataws and Cherokees and Mohawks and Miamis, Schenectaws and Catabaws with the Sachems and their Squaws,
Oh, what a fight it was to see, what a din, what a glorious rattle!
And I so snugly perched up in a tree, had a bird's eye view of the battle.

"It is said that the Cherokee chorus was one of the grandest ever composed; the effect was sublime." (Michael Kelly in his *Reminiscences*)

The Cherokee was produced in Boston, June 24, 1799. It was revived in London in 1802 with additional music by Michael Kelly, under the title *Algonah.*

Storace's *The Iron Chest* is not an American subject.

STRUBE, GUSTAV (1867 - 1953)

The Captive Baltimore, Feb. 28, 1938

Libretto in three acts by Frederic Arnold Kummer; formerly entitled *Ramona.* Produced by the Baltimore Civic Opera Company.

Action is in the town of Port Royal, Jamaica, West Indies, at the close of the 17th century. The characters are Spaniards, Negroes, mulattos, and early New England buccaneers, slaves, citizens, sailors, and traders. There are no Indians. Mr. Kummer's play ran on Broadway many years ago as a vehicle for Florence Reed.

The original score is in the library of Peabody Institute, Baltimore.

SURETTE, THOMAS WHITNEY (1861 - 1941)

Priscilla; or, The Pilgrim's Proxy Concord, Mass., Mar. 6, 1888

Libretto by Henry D. Coolidge after Longfellow. This work is intended for amateurs or semi-professional groups. It had over 1000 performances in the United States.

Vocal score published by Boston Music Co., 1889.

TANNER, Mrs. F. G.

Watouska; or, The White Lily

Mrs. Tanner was a resident of St. Louis, but no further information is available..

TAYLOR, RAYNOR (c. 1747 - 1825)

The American Tar; or, The Press Gang Defeated

A successful ballad opera containing the song "Independent and Free," published about 1812.

Pizarro; or, The Spaniards in Peru Philadelphia, 1800

Incidental music for the play composed in collaboration with Alexander Reinagle.

TERRASSE, CLAUDE (1867 - 1923)

Les Transatlantiques Paris, May 20, 1911

Libretto in three acts by Hermant and Franc-Nohain; this is a musical comedy with scenes in Newport and New York.

Vocal score published by Eschig, 1911.

THOMSON, VIRGIL (1896 -)

The Mother of Us All **New York, May 7, 1947**

Libretto in three acts by Gertrude Stein and the composer; scenario by Maurice Grosser. The subject is Susan B. Anthony and friends, the winning of political rights for women in the United States. Historical figures make their appearances: John Quincy Adams, U. S. Grant, Daniel Webster, Andrew Johnson, and — Lillian Russell.

Commissioned by the Alice M. Ditson Fund, this work received nine performances at Columbia University. Vocal score published by Music Press, 1947.

Revived in 1956 at the Phoenix Theater, New York. "Aging rapidly," wrote Howard Taubman of *The New York Times.* "It still has an air of smartness, but the slickness and foolishness were shining through."

TONNING, GERARD (1860 - 1940)

Leif Erikson **Seattle, Dec. 10, 1910**

Three acts. Text in Norwegian by C. M. Thuland; the scene is Vineland (America) and Greenland in 1001 B.C. Also given in Brooklyn on Oct. 4, 1924; both performances in Norwegian.

In Old New England

Dramatic sketch; text by Sarah Pratt Carr. The time is 1840, and the work includes authentic Colonial songs.

TRITTO, GIACOMO (1733 - 1824)

Gli Americani **Naples, Nov. 4, 1802**

Libretto in two acts by G. Rossi. A new version, entitled *Gonzalvo,* was offered in 1805.

VALLE-RIESTRA, JOSÉ MARÍA (1859 - 1925)

Ollanta **Lima, Dec. 26, 1900**

An Inca subject. Story in Martens. Duet for soprano and mezzo-soprano published, Lima, 193-. This is the first native Peruvian opera, and is based on authentic Incan melodies.

Las Rosas de Jamaica

Opera in one act, on an Inca subject.

Atahualpa

Opera in three acts on an Inca subject; only one act completed.

VAN BROEKHOVEN, JOHN (1856 - 1930)

A Colonial Wedding Cincinnati, 1905

Puritan subject in one act.

VAN BUSKIRK, CARL G. (1907 -)

The Land between the Rivers St. Louis, 1956

In two acts, based on Robert Penn Warren's *The Ballad of Billie Potts.*

VASSILENKO, SERGEY (1872 - 1956)

Christopher Columbus

Composed in 1933; never produced.

VENTH, CARL (1860 - 1938)

La Vida de la Misión San Antonio, Texas, 1959

Libretto by the composer on an Indian uprising in 1750 against the San José Mission, San Antonio.

This work was intended for the Texas Centennial Exposition of 1935, but was not produced owing to lack of funds. For twenty years thereafter, Mrs. Venth, a Norwegian-born musician, and long-time piano teacher in San Antonio, tried to find support for a full-scale production. She was without family, and her life-savings, amounting to $55,000, were sufficient. After her death, the work, by previous arrangement with her bank, was produced with Emile Renan conducting the San Antonio Symphony.

Musicians considered the work to be expertly scored, well written for the voice, melodious, and dramatically effective. The style is somewhat out of fashion, and the language of the text a bit high-flown. There are Puccinian flavors.

Mr. Venth also wrote *The Rebel,* a fairy opera with dance (Fort Worth, May 29, 1926).

VERDI, GUISEPPE (1813 - 1901)

Un Ballo in maschera Rome, Feb. 17, 1859

Libretto in three acts by A. Somma, based on Scribe's libretto for Auber's

Gustav III. At the last moment censorship necessitated a change of locale, and Boston, in Puritan times, was substituted for Naples. Characters include Riccardo, Governor of Boston, Reinhart, a Creole, his Secretary, and Ulrica, a black astrologer. Riccardo dies, sincerely mourned by his people, who loved him like a father.

Produced in New York, Feb. 11, 1861, in Italian, Feb. 5, 1871, in English, and Dec. 11, 1889, in German.

Vocal score published by Ricordi, 1859.

VIDAL Y CARETAS

Cristobal Colon **Barcelona, Sept. 1892**

VILLA-LOBOS, HEITOR (1887 - 1959)

Malazarte **Rio de Janeiro, 1921**

Libretto in three acts by Graça Aranha, the same as that used by other composers.

VILLANI, ANGELO (1821 - 1863)

La Spia; ossia, il mercaiuolo americano **Turin, 1850**

See Arditi's work on the same subject.

VILLATA, GASPAR (1851 - 1891)

Cristobal Colombo **Genoa**

Libretto by A. de Lauzières in three acts, Act III taking place in Cuba. See Tolón and González for further details.

VINATIERI, FELIX (c. 1834 -)

The American Volunteer **(One act only) Yankton, S. D., Mar. 4, 1961**

Opera in four acts with libretto by the composer, "an odd reworking of the Faust legend, with bits of the Rip van Winkle tale, and a snatch of *Paradise Lost* in reverse." Claimed to be the first opera composed west of the Mississippi, c. 1889. This work was produced by faculty members, students, and townfolk of Yankton under the direction of Latien Weed.

Yankton was the western rail terminus where General Custer arrived on his way to defeat by Sitting Bull in 1873.

The American Volunteer is a soldier in Washington's army who sells his soul to the Devil to avoid disgrace; he goes to Hell for a decade but awakes a century later to stage a successful rebellion in that fiery region.

In the music there is an obvious debt to Verdi, a great deal of Bizet (including a Habanera with castanets), Donizetti and Rossini also taking bows, and Strauss (Johann) being present in marches and dances. Vinatieri's own style is identifiable, however; it is vigorous and inciting to stomping and laughter, according to the Yankton critic, James Boeringer. "The music is ingratiating, propulsive and tuneful, and the plot hilariously funny," he writes.

Vinatieri was born in Turin, came to America in 1859 after six years study at the Naples Conservatory, and signed as bandmaster throughout the Civil War for the Sixteenth Infantry of Boston and the Twenty-Second Infantry of Fort Columbus, New York. The latter assignment sent him to Fort Sully in South Dakota, where he was mustered out of the Army. Boating down the Mississippi toward New Orleans, he decided on Yankton. There he led the forces which met to greet Gen. Custer, liked the man, and became his bandmaster.

In addition to *The American Volunteer* there are two one-act operas, works whose pages may have contributed to this one: *One Summer in Texas, Heart and Love,* and *The Barber of the Reggement (sic)* which is full-length. Prof. Weed made a full score from assembled parts, providing a second violin part which was missing. See article in *The New York Times,* April 2, 1961.

WALD, MAX (1889 - 1954)

A Provincial Episode; or, Gay Little World Athens, Ohio, July 17, 1952

Chamber opera in one act, one scene, with libretto by the composer; set in a small Midwestern town in the 1890's. The performance at Ohio University was given with two pianos; it is not certain whether there is an orchestration. The vocal score is in the University's library. Wald taught at Chicago College of Music, now part of Roosevelt University.

WALLACE, WILLIAM VINCENT (1812 - 1865)

The Desert Flower London, Oct. 12, 1863

A ballad opera in the style of Balfe; three acts with text by G. A. Harris and J. T. Williams, based on *Jaguarita l'Indienne* by J. H. Vernoy de Saint-Georges and A. deLeuven. Subject: New Guinea Papuans.

Produced in New York Jan. 15, 1868.

Vocal score published by Hall, 1869.

WARD, ROBERT (1917 -)

The Crucible New York, Oct. 26, 1961

An opera in three acts, libretto by Bernard Stambler, based on the play of the same title by Arthur Miller. Subject: Witchhunts in 17th-century Salem, Mass.

Produced with a grant from the Ford Foundation. The cast of the City Center Opera included Patricia Brooks, Francis Bible, Debra Brown, Eunice Alberts, Norman Kelly, Paul Ukena, Norman Treigle.

"Mr. Ward uses . . . a harmonic language based on 19th century procedures — a completely non-dissonant language. It is indicative of the current neo-romantic trend in composition. Ten years ago the chances are that a composer would have been laughed out of court had so 'old-fashioned' a work been presented.

"Mr. Miller's play is a powerful work, and has been adapted virtually intact. The action was strong enough to come right through Mr. Ward's frequently noncommittal music. For noncommittal the music was, and it did little to intensify the characters on stage, the moods they were feeling, or the situations in which they found themselves." (Harold C. Schonberg, *The New York Times,* Oct. 28, 1961)

"The libretto follows the play closely, much dialogue being set to music intact, and it generates a power in the theater to which the music of Mr. Robert Ward definitely contributes. It is music for orchestra as well as voice, with some instrumental felicities in suggesting the Massachusetts spring and rising with some richness of vocal part-writing to the play's dramatic climaxes. . . . *The Crucible* takes the stage with a dynamic force that may well drive it into the international repertory." (*The Times,* London, April 2, 1962)

WARE, HARRIET (1877 - 1962)

Priscilla

Mentioned by Hipsher; no futher information.

WEIL, OSCAR (1840 - 1921)

In Mexico

WEILL, KURT (1900 - 1950)

Aufstieg und Fall der Stadt Mahogonny — **Baden-Baden, July 17, 1927**

Singspiel, or work with spoken dialogue. The city of Mahagonny is fictionally located on the Gold Coast of California; the characters are escapees from a penal colony. The work caused an artistic scandal.

Vocal score published by Universal-Edition, 1929.

Aufstieg und Fall der Stadt Mahagonny — **Leipzig, March 9, 1930**

Text in three acts by Bertold Brecht. This is a full-length work developed from the above. The leading character is named Jimmy Mahoney.

"There is no such thing or place as Mahagonny. Mahagonny is an imaginary city of the wild west near the Gold Coast. It is a city which is today founded by three scamps, a procuress, a rowdy, a cut-throat, and which tomorrow will disappear. It is a city which offers to all vagabonds and gentry who earn and spend more quickly than they require: wine, women, and song: gambling and fighting. One thing only is taboo — to be without money.

"*Mahagonny* is an opera which belongs to no opera house. It is an opera which deviates from all accepted features of operatic style and one which breaks with all accepted features of operatic illusion, with the requirements of beautiful melody and, above all, with the canons of art. It was a mistake to mount it in a modern opera house.

"The symbolism becomes more and more exaggerated until the whole amounts to nothing more than a demonstration against capitalism." (Alfred Einstein)

"Another and more surprising aspect struck me during the evening, namely, the rapidity with which the piece has aged during its 18 months of existence, so much so that it appears in the light of an antique." (Walter Schrenk in *The Christian Science Monitor)*

Down in the Valley — **Bloomington, Indiana, July 14, 1945**

A folk opera in one act with libretto by Arnold Sundgaard, conceived for production by non-professional groups. The score makes use of five well-known folk songs. Vocal score published by G. Schirmer, 1948. First produced at Indiana University with a cast of students.

Knickerbocker Holiday — **Hartford, Conn., Sept. 26, 1938**

Text in two acts by Maxwell Anderson. This work is considered a musical comedy, although it is similar in technique to *Mahagonny*. It was the first of Weill's scores written and produced in America. Walter Huston sang (?) the leading role.

Collection of songs published by Crawford, 1938.

Street Scene — **New York, Jan. 9, 1947**

From the play of the same name by Elmer Rice, with lyrics by Langston Hughes. Three acts. The score contains such unusual numbers as an "ice cream sextet," "trio of gossips," "School girl's song," and duet of two children reading a newspaper. The cast included Polyna Stoska, Brian Sullivan, and Anne Jeffreys.

Vocal score published by Chappell, 1948. Produced in Düsseldorf, 1955.

"Obviously this is the theme he [Weill] has been waiting for to make full use of his maturity as composer." *(New York Times)* "Here is a modern opera which is not to be dismissed lightly." *(New York Herald-Tribune)*

WEINBERGER, JAROMIR (1896 -)

Lidé z Pokerflatu — **Brno, Nov. 19, 1932**

Five acts. Text by Milos Kares, after Bret Harte's *The Outcasts of Poker Flat.*

WHITE, CLARENCE CAMERON (1880 - 1960)

Ouanga — **New York, 1956**

Libretto by John F. Matheus follows the story of Jean-Jacques Dessalines, the slave who led his people in revolt and became Emperor of Haiti at the beginning of the 19th century. The theme of the opera is the attempt of Dessalines to eliminate Voodooism from Haitian thought.

Excerpts were performed on Nov. 13, 1932, in Chicago.

MacHenry Boatwright sang the lead; a large chorus sat at the rear of the stage in concert style. The work was considered to have attractive music, but quite lacking in tension. Sung at the Metropolitan Opera House.

Vocal score published by Sam Fox Publishing Co., 1955.

WHITELY, BESSIE W. (1871 -)

Sarita

A grand opera on a Mexican subject based on an original libretto by the composer. Mrs. Whitely lived in St. Louis.

WILDER, ALEC (1907 -)

Wilder is the composer of a number of short works designed for performance in schools, such as his one-act operas *Sunday Excursion* (1953) and *The Lowland Sea* 1951; Arnold Sundgaard is librettist in both instances.

WINTER, PETER VON (1754 - 1825)

Das unterbrochene Opferfest — Vienna, June 14, 1796

The Interrupted Sacrifice has a text by F. X. Huber, and is in two acts. Subject: the Incas in Peru. Apparently never produced in the United States, but one of the most successful operas in Europe between the time of *Die Zauberflöte* and *Der Freischütz.*

Copy of vocal score in manuscript, Boston Public Library.

YORK, FRANCIS L. (1861 - 1955)

The Inca

A comic opera in manuscript.

ZECH, FREDERICK, JR. (1858 - 1926)

La Paloma

Libretto by Mary Fairweather. Score lost.

Wa-Kin-Yon; or, The Passing of the Red Men

Libretto in three acts by Mary Fairweather. Written about 1914 but unproduced.

ZINGARELLI, NICOLA ANTONIO (1752 - 1837)

Montesuma — Naples, Aug. 13, 1781

Libretto in three acts by V. A. Cigna-Santi. Haydn praised the work highly.

Carolina e Mexico — Venice, 1798

TOPICS

AND

LOCALES

SPANISH-AMERICAN SUBJECTS

Argentina

Berutti, Arturo	Pampa
Boero, Felipe	Tucumán
"	Raquela
Bonicioli, Fruhman Ricardo	Don Juan de Garay
Rogatis, Pascual de	Huemac

Brazil

Braga, Francisco	Jupira
Carvalho, Eleazar de	Descuberta do Brasil
"	Tiradentes
David, Félicien	La Perle du Brésil
Fernândez, Oscar Lorenzo	Malazarte
Gomes, Antonio Carlos	Il Guarany
Guarnieri, Camargo	Malazarte
Lobo, Elias Alvares	A Noite de São João
Mignone, Francisco	O Contratador dos Diamantes
Pereira, Elpidio	Calabar
Villa-Lobos, Heitor	Malazarte

Chile

Gajardo, Remigio Acevedo	Caupolicán
Marqués y García, Pedro Miguel	La Monja Alférez
Ortíz de Zárate, Eliodoro	La Fiorista di Lugano

Mexico

Arnold, Samuel	New Spain; or, Love in Mexico
Bishop, Henry Rowley	Cortez; or, The Conquest of Mexico
Fanciulli, Francesco	Malinche; or, The Day of Sacrifice
Floridia, Pietro	La Colonia libera
Freeman, Harry L.	Valdo
"	Vendetta
Gleason, Frederick Grant	Montezuma
Graun, Karl H.	Montezuma
Hadley, Henry	Azora, Daughter of Montezuma
Jones, Abbie Gerrish	The Aztec Princess
Kerrison, Davenport	The Last of the Aztecs
Majo, Giovanni	Montezuma
Milhaud, Darius	Maximilien
Müller, Wenzel	Vitzilipututzli
Mysliveček, Josef	Motezuma
Ortega, Aniceto	Guatimozin
Portogallo, Marcos	Fernando nel Messico
Ricci, Luigi	L'eroina del Messico
Rogatis, Pascual de	Huemac
Sessions, Roger	Montezuma

Spontini, Gasparo	Fernand Cortez; ou, la Conquête du Mexique
Stewart, Humphrey John	Montezuma
Weil, Oscar	In Mexico
Whitely, Bessie W.	Sarita
Zingarelli, Nicola Antonio	Carolina e Mexico
"	Montesuma

Peru

Anonymous	The Cruelty of the Spaniards in Peru
Berners, Lord	Le Carrosse du Saint-Sacrement
Berutti, Arturo	Yupanky
Bishop, Henry Rowley	The Virgin of the Sun
Candeille, Pierre Joseph	Pizarre; ou, la Conquête du Pérou
Cimarosa, Domenico	Le Vergine del sole
Dussek, Jan Ladislav	Pizarro
Haan, Willem de	Die Inkasöhne
Hatton, John Liptrott	Pizarro
Hewitt, James	Pizarro; or, The Spanish in Peru
Hook, James	The Fair Peruvian
Hugo, John Adam	The Sun God
Hummel, Ferdinand	Assarpai
Kelly, Michael	Pizarro
Linley ,Thomas	Pizarro
Lortzing, Gustav Albert	Die Schatzkammer des Inka
Marqués y García, Pedro Miguel	La Monja Alférez
Méhul, Étienne	Alonzo et Cora
Müller, Wenzel	Die Prinzessin von Kakambo
Offenbach, Jacques	La Périchole
Reinagle, Alexander	Pizarro; or, The Spaniards in Peru
Republicano, Antonio	Amasonas
Rolla, Alessandro	Pizarro; o, la conquista del Peru
Schroeder, Hermann	Pizarro; oder, Die Eroberung von Peru
Taylor, Raynor	Pizarro; or, The Spaniards in Peru
Valle-Riestra, José María	Ollanta
"	Atahualpa
"	Las Rosas de Jamaica
Winter, Peter von	Das unterbrochene Opferfest
York, Francis L.	The Inca

Other Spanish-American Subjects

Balfe, Michael William	The Maid of Artois
Battista, Vincenzo	Il Corsaro della Guadalupa
Benoist, François	Nisida; ou, les Amazons des Açores
Converse, Frederick S.	The Sacrifice
De Campos, Carlos	Un Caso singolare
Delius, Frederick	Koanga (Louisiana)
Donizetti, Gaetano	Il Furioso nell' Isola di San Domingo
Egk, Werner	Die Verlobung in San Domingo
Falla, Manuel de	La Atlántida

Houseley, Henry	Ponce de León
Jongen, Léon	Thomas l'Agnelet, Gentilhomme de Fortune
Listov, Konstantin	Cuba's Daughter
Maeder, James Gaspard	Ponce de León
Mattausch, Albert	Die Jassabraut
Mauri, José	La Esclava
Milhaud, Darius	Bolivar
Moncada, Bernardo	Teresa
Offenbach, Jacques	La Créole
Ortíz de Zárate, Eliodoro	Lautaro
Petrella, Errico	I Pirati spagnuoli
Spelman, Timothy Mather	La Magnifica
Still, William Grant	Troubled Island
Strube, Gustav	The Captive (Jamaica, West Indies)
Venth, Carl	La Vida de la Misión
White, Clarence Cameron	Ouanga (Haiti)
Zech, Frederick, Jr.	La Paloma

INDIAN SUBJECTS

Adam, Adolphe	Les Mohicans
Albright, Lois	Hopitu (Hopi)
Allen, Paul Hastings	The Last of the Mohicans (Huron and Delaware)
Arditi, Luigi	La Spia
Arnold, Samuel	Inkle and Yarico
Berutti, Arturo	Yupanky (Inca)
Bimboni, Alberto	Winona (Chippewa, Sioux)
Blakeslee, E. Earle	The Legend of Wiwaste
Bray, John	The Indian Princess
Cadman, Charles Wakefield	Daoma
"	Shanewis
"	The Sunset Trail
Castro, Herrera	Atzimba (Aztec)
Colburn, George	The Masque of Montezuma (Aztec)
Converse, Frederick	The Sacrifice
David, Félicien	La Perle du Brésil
Davis, A. J.	The Last of the Mohicans
De Leone, Francesco	Alglala
Fanciulli, Francesco	Malinche
Farner, Eugene A.	The White Buffalo Maiden (Sioux)
Fomin, Yevstigney	Amerikantsy
Freer, Eleanor E.	The Chilkoot Maiden
Gabrielli, Nicolo	L'Americano in fiera
Gajardo, Remigio	Caupolicán
Genée, Franz	Die letzten Mohikaner
Gleason, Frederick Grant	Montezuma
Gomes, Antonio Carlos	Il Guarany (Amazon)
Graun, Karl H.	Montezuma
Grétry, André	Le Huron
Haan, Willem de	Die Inkasöhne

Hadley, Henry K.	Azora, Daughter of Montezuma
Halévy, Jacques	Jaguarita l'Indienne (Pawnee)
Hanson, William	The Sun Dance (Sioux)
"	Tam-Man-Nacup
Herbert, Victor	Natoma
Hewitt, James	Tammany (Delaware)
Hook, James	The Fair Peruvian (Inca)
Hugo, John Adam	The Sun God (Inca)
Hummel, Ferdinand	Assarpai (Inca)
Hyde, F. S.	Title unknown
Jones, Abbie Gerrish	The Aztec Princess
Kauer, Ferdinand	Inkle und Yariko
Kelly, Michael	The Indian
Kerrison, Davenport	The Last of the Aztecs
King, Matthew Peter	The Americans
Knowlton, E. Bruce	Wakuta
Lieurance, Thurlow	Drama of the Yellowstone
Lortzing, Gustav	Die Schatzkammer des Inka (Inca)
Majo, Giovanni	Montezuma
Méhul, Étienne	Alonzo et Cora (Inca)
Moore, Mary Carr	The Flaming Arrow
"	Narcissa
"	Los Rubios
Müller, Wenzel	Die Prinzessin von Kakambo (Inca)
"	Vitzilipututzli
Mysliveček, Josef	Motezuma
Nevin, Arthur	Poia (Blackfoot)
Ortega, Aniceto	Guatimotzin (Aztec)
Ortíz de Zárate, Eliodoro	Lautaro (Araucanian)
Patton, Willard	Pocahontas
Phelps, Ellsworth C.	The Last of the Mohicans
Piccini, Niccolò	L'Americano ingentilito
Purcell, Henry	The Indian Queen (Aztec)
Republicano, Antonio	Amasonas (Inca)
Rogatis, Pascual de	Huemac (Chibcha)
Sánchez de Fuentes, Eduardo	Doreya
Schoenefeld, Henry	Atala
Skilton, Charles S.	Bluefeather (Pueblo)
"	Kalopin (Chickasaw, Choctaw)
"	The Sun Bride
Sobolewski, Eduard de	Mohega
Southard, Lucien H.	Omano
Storace, Stephen	The Cherokee
Tanner, F. G.	Watouska
Valle-Riestra, José María	Ollanta (Inca)
"	Atahualpa (Inca)
Venth, Carl	La Vida de la Misión
Villani, Angelo	La Spia
Wallace, William Vincent	The Desert Flower
Winter, Peter von	Das unterbrochene Opferfest (Inca)
York, Francis	The Inca
Zech, Frederick, Jr.	Wa-Kin-Yon

SUBJECTS FROM AMERICAN AND ENGLISH LITERATURE

Louisa May Alcott

Freer, Eleanor Everest	Little Women

Stephen Vincent Benét

Moore, Douglas	The Devil and Daniel Webster

James Fenimore Cooper

Adam, Adolphe	Les Mohicans
Allen, Paul Hastings	The Last of the Mohicans
Arditi, Luigi	La Spia
Davis, A. J.	The Last of the Mohicans
Genée, Franz	Die letzten Mohikaner
Halévy, Jacques	Jaguarita l'Indienne (The Spy)
Phelps, E. C.	The Last of the Mohicans
Planquette, Jean-Robert	Surcouf (The Pilot)
Villani, Angelo	La Spia

Daniel Defoe

Barbieri, Francisco	Robinson Crusoe
Dalayrac, Nicolas	Azémia; ou, Le nouveau Robinson
Fioravanti, Vincenzo	Robinson Crusoe
Linley, Thomas	Robinson Crusoe
Offenbach, Jacques	Robinson Crusoé

Edward Everett Hale

Damrosch, Walter	The Man Without a Country

Bret Harte

Floridia, Pietro	La Colonia libera (M'Liss)
Weinberger, Jaromir	Lidé z Pokerflatu (The Outcasts of Poker Flat)

Nathaniel Hawthorne

Carlson, Charles F.	Hester; or, The Scarlet Letter
Claflin, Avery	Hester Prynne
Damrosch, Walter	The Scarlet Letter
Floridia, Pietro	The Scarlet Letter
Giannini, Vittorio	The Scarlet Letter
Kaufmann, Walter	The Scarlet Letter
Southard, Lucien H.	The Scarlet Letter

Dorothy and DuBose Heywood

Gershwin, George	Porgy and Bess

Washington Irving

Bristow, George F.	Rip van Winkle
De Koven, Reginald	Rip van Winkle
(Jordan, Jules	Rip van Winkle)
Leoni, Franco	Rip van Winkle
Manning, Edward B.	Rip van Winkle
Maretzek, Max	Sleepy Hollow; or, The Headless Horseman
Moore, Douglas	The Headless Horseman; or, A Legend of Sleepy Hollow
Planquette, Jean-Robert	Rip van Winkle

Henry James

Moore, Douglas	Wings of the Dove

Henry Wadsworth Longfellow

Carlson, Charles F.	The Courtship of Miles Standish
Eames, Henry Purmort	Priscilla
Fanciulli, Francesco	Priscilla; or, The Maid of Plymouth
Jones, Abbie Gerrish	Priscilla
Leroux, Xavier	Évangeline
Luening, Otto	Evangeline
Rice, Edward E.	Evangeline
Spelman, Timothy Mather	The Courtship of Miles Standish
Surette, Thomas Whitney	Priscilla; or, The Pilgrim's Proxy
Ware, Harriet	Priscilla

Arthur Miller

Ward, Robert	The Crucible

Eugene O'Neill

Gruenberg, Louis	The Emperor Jones

Gertrude Stein

Thomson, Virgil	The Mother of Us All

Harriet Beecher Stowe

Ferrari-Trecate, Luigi	La Capanna dello zio Tom
Florio, Caryl	Uncle Tom's Cabin
Giorza, Paolo	La Capanna dello zio Tom

Mark Twain (Samuel Clemens)

Foss, Lukas	The Jumping Frog of Calaveras County

John Greenleaf Whittier

Bonner, Eugene	Barbara Frietchie (from the play by Clyde Fitch)

SUBJECT: AMERICAN REVOLUTION

Anonymous	Americania and Elutheria; or, A New Tale of the Genii
Anonymous	Federation Triumphant in the Steady Hearts of Connecticut Alone; or, The Turnpike Road to a Fortune
Anonymous	Yankee Chronology; or, Huzza for the Constitution
Arditi, Luigi	La Spia
Coerne, Louis Adolphe	A Woman of Marblehead
Damrosch, Walter	The Man Without a Country
Pelissier, Victor	The Launch; or, Huzza for the Constitution
Sobolewski, Eduard de	Mohega; or, The Flower of the Forest
Villani, Angelo	La Spia

SUBJECT: CIVIL WAR

Dello Joio, Norman	Blood Moon
Floyd, Carlisle	The Passion of Jonathan Wade
Kreutz, Arthur	The University Greys
Lockwood, Normand	Early Dawn
Moross, Jerome	Gentlemen, Be Seated!
Nevin, Arthur	A Daughter of the Forest

SUBJECT: COLUMBUS

Anonymous	Columbus; or, The Discovery of America
"	The Story of Columbus
Barbieri, Carlo Emmanuele di	Cristoforo Colombo
Bottesini, Giovanni	Cristoforo Colombo
Carnicer, Ramón	Cristóforo Colón
Casella, Donna Felicita	Cristoforo Colombo
Coppola, Pietro Antonio	Cristoforo Colombo
Egk, Werner	Christopher Columbus
Fabrizi, Vincenzo	Il Colombo
Fava, Alessandro	Il Colombo
Ferreira, D.	Columbus
Fioravanti, Vincenzo	Colombo alla scoperta delle Indie
Franchetti, Alberto	Cristoforo Colombo
Giambini	Il Colombo
Hewitt, James	Columbus
Llanos y Bereta, A.	Colombo
Marcora, C.	Cristoforo Colombo
Mela, Vincenzo	Cristoforo Colombo
Milhaud, Darius	Christophe Colomb
Moore, Homer	Columbus; or, The New World
Morales, Julio Melesio	Cristoforo Colombo a San Domingo

Morlacchi, Francesco	Colombo
Ottoboni, Pietro	Il Colombo; ossia, l'India scoperta
Pelissier, Victor	Columbus; or, The Discovery of America
Pignani, Enrico	Cristoforo Colombo
Pratt, Silas Gamaliel	The Triumph of Columbus
Rabiti, Sangiorgio	Il Colombo
Reinagle, Alexander	Columbus; or, A World Discovered
Ricci, Luigi	Il Colombo
Vassilenko, Sergey	Christopher Columbus
Vidal y Caretas	Cristobal Colon
Villata, Gaspar	Cristobal Colombo

SUBJECT: MORMONS

Brandl, Johann	Die Mormonen
Buck, Dudley	Deseret; or, A Saint's Affliction
Kastle, Leonard	Deseret

SUBJECT: RACE RELATIONS

Dello Joio, Norman	Blood Moon
Jones, Daniel	The Knife
Meyerowitz, Jan	The Barrier

SUBJECT: SALEM, MASSACHUSETTS

(See *also:* Hawthorne, Nathaniel)

Appleton, Adeline Carola	The Witches' Well
Cadman, Charles Wakefield	A Witch of Salem
Kelley, Edgar Stillman	Puritania; or, The Earl and the Maid of Salem
Jones, Abbie Gerrish	Priscilla (probably Salem)
Lockwood, Normand	The Scarecrow
Moore, Homer	The Puritans
Ward, Robert	The Crucible

RURAL NORTH AMERICAN SUBJECTS

Composer	Work
Anonymous	Federation Triumphant in the Steady Hearts of Connecticut Alone
Anonymous	Yankee Chronology; or, Huzza for the Constitution (New York State)
Bacon, Ernst	A Tree on the Plains (Southwest)
Beach, L.	Jonathan Postfree; or, The Honest Yankee
Beeson, Jack	The Sweet Bye and Bye (Arkansas)
"	Hello Out There (Texas)
Bezanson, Philip	Golden Child (California)
Bucharoff, Simon	The Lover's Knot (Norfolk, Virginia)
Carter, Ernest Trow	The Blonde Donna; or, The Fiesta of Santa Barbara (California)
"	The White Bird (Upper New York State)
Coerne, Louis Adolphe	A Woman of Marblehead (Massachusetts)
Cole, Rossetter G.	The Maypole Lovers (Quincy, Massachusetts)
Copland, Aaron	The Tender Land (Midwest)
Davies, John	The Forest Rose; or, The American Farmers
Edwards, Robert	Tennessee
Enna, Emil	The Dawn of the West
Faetkenhauer, Max	Amelia Mora (Wisconsin)
Fink, Myron	Jeremiah (Illinois)
"	Susanna and the Elders (Tennessee)
Floyd, Carlisle	Susannah (Tennessee)
"	The Passion of Jonathan Wade (Southern United States)
"	The Sojourner and Mollie Sinclair (North Carolina)
Foss, Lukas	The Jumping Frog of Calaveras County (Missouri)
Freeman, Harry L.	The Plantation (Southern United States)
"	The Tryst (Southern Michigan)
Freer, Eleanor Everest	The Chilkoot Maiden (Alaska)
Giannini, Vittorio	The Harvest (Southwest)
Halévy, Jacques	L'Éclair (Boston, Massachusetts)
Hall, William John	Louisiana
Hanson, Howard	Merry Mount (Quincy, Massachusetts)
Harling, W. Franke	A Light from St. Agnes (Louisiana)
"	Deep River (Southern United States)
Haufrecht, Herbert	Boney Quillen (Upper New York State)
Hawkins, Micah	The Saw Mill; or, A Yankee Trick
Jones, Daniel	The Knife (Southern United States)
Joplin, Scott	Treemonisha (Arkansas)
Kastle, Leonard	Deseret (Utah)
Knowlton, E. Bruce	The Woodsman (Pacific Northwest)
"	Montana
Lockwood, Normand	Early Dawn (Illinois)
Menotti, Gian-Carlo	The Old Maid and the Thief (West Chester, Pennsylvania)
Meyerowitz, Jan	The Barrier (Georgia)
"	Eastward in Eden (Amherst, Massachusetts)

Minschull, John	Rural Felicity
Moore, Douglas	The Devil and Daniel Webster (New Hampshire)
"	Giants in the Earth (Dakotah territory)
"	The Headless Horseman (Upper New York State)
Nevin, Arthur	A Daughter of the Forest (Western Pennsylvania)
Root, George F.	The Haymakers
Smith, David Stanley	Merry Mount (Quincy, Massachusetts)
Still, William Grant	A Southern Interlude
"	A Bayou Legend (Louisiana)
Van Broekhoven, John	A Colonial Wedding
Van Buskirk, Carl G.	The Land Between the Rivers
Vinatieri, Felix	The American Volunteer (South Dakota)
Wald, Max	A Provincial Episode
Ward, Robert	The Crucible (Salem, Massachusetts)
Weill, Kurt	Down in the Valley

URBAN NORTH AMERICAN SUBJECTS

Anonymous	May Day in Town; or, New York in an Uproar
Antheil, George	Transatlantic; or, The People's Choice
"	The Wish (Greenwich Village, New York City)
Bennett, Robert Russell	Maria Malibran (New York)
Bimboni, Alberto	In the Name of Culture
Blitzstein, Marc	Regina (Virginia)
Brand, Max	Maschinist Hopkins
Carey, S.	True Blue (The Battery, New York City)
Case, Henry Lincoln	Hinotito; A Romance of Love and Politics
Chadwick, George Whitefield	The Padrone (East Coast port)
Converse, Frederick S.	The Immigrants (The Battery, New York City)
Damrosch, Walter	The Dove of Peace (New Hampshire; Washington, D. C.)
Dello Joio, Norman	Blood Moon (New Orleans, Paris, New York)
Freeman, Harry L.	The Flapper (New York City)
Gershwin, George	Porgy and Bess (South Carolina)
Giannini, Vittorio	Rehearsal Call (New York City)
Hewitt, James	Tammany (New York City)
Krenek, Ernst	Jonny spielt auf
Leoni, Franco	L'Oracolo (San Francisco)
Maryon, Edward	The Smelting Pot (East Side, New York City)
"	The Werewolf (Quincy, Massachusetts)
Mendelssohn, Felix	Die beiden Neffen; oder, Der Onkel aus Boston

Menotti, Gian-Carlo	Le dernier Sauvage (Chicago)
"	The Saint of Bleecker Street (East Side, New York City)
Moore, Douglas	The Ballad of Baby Doe (Colorado; Washington, D. C.)
"	White Wings (New York City)
"	Wings of the Dove (London; Venice)
Patterson, Franklin P.	A Little Girl at Play
Pelissier, Victor	The Fourth of July; or, Temple of American Independence (Battery, Broadway, New York City)
Ralph, James	The Launch; or, Huzza for the Constitution (Charlestown, Massachusetts)
"	The Disappointment; or, The Force of Credulity (Philadelphia)
Rossini, Gioacchino A.	La Cambiale di matrimonio (London)
Schuman, William	The Mighty Casey ("Mudville, U. S. A.")
Thomson, Virgil	The Mother of Us All
Weill, Kurt	Aufstieg und Fall der Stadt Mahagonny (California)
"	Knickerbocker Holiday (New Amsterdam)
"	Street Scene (New York City)

INDEX OF TITLES

GENERAL INDEX

SELECTIVE BIBLIOGRAPHY

CHAMPLIN, J. D., Jr.: *Cyclopedia of Music and Musicians* (New York: Scribner, 1888)

HIPSHER, Edward E.: *American Opera and Its Composers* (Philadelphia: Presser, 1954)

HOWARD, John Tasker: *Our American Music,* 4th revised ed. (New York: Crowell, 1954)

———: *Our Contemporary Composers* (New York: Crowell, 1948)

KROHN, Ernst: *A Century of Missouri Music* (St. Louis: privately printed, 1924)

LOEWENBERG, Alfred: *Annals of Opera, 1597-1940* (Cambridge, England: Heffer, 1943; new edition, Geneva: Societas Bibliographica, 1955)

MARTENS, Frederick: *One Thousand and One Nights of Opera* (New York: Appleton, 1926, 1938)

MATTFELD, Julius: *A Hundred Years of Grand Opera in New York* (New York Public Library, 1927)

ODELL, George C.: *Annals of the New York Stage* (New York: Columbia University Press, 1927-1949)

SCHATZ, Albert: *Catalogue of Opera Librettos Printed before 1800,* prepared by O. G. Sonneck, 2 vols. (Washington, D. C.: Library of Congress, 1914)

SLONIMSKY, Nicolas: *Music of Latin America* (New York: Crowell, 1945)

———: *Music Since 1900,* 3d ed. (New York: Coleman-Ross, 1949)

SONNECK, Oscar G.: *Early Opera in America* (New York: G. Schirmer, 1915)

———: *Miscellaneous Studies in the History of Music* (New York: Macmillan, 1921)

TOLÓN, Edward, and GONZÁLEZ, Jorge: *Óperas Cubanas y sus autores* (Havana, 1943)

TOWERS, John: *Dictionary-Catalogue of Upwards of 28,000 Operas and Operettas which have been performed on the Public Stage from Earliest Times to the Present* (Morgantown, W. Va.: Acme Publishing Co., 1910)

Coleman-Ross Books on Music

The Design and Composition for this book
by Wilder's Trade Comps, Fitchburg, Mass.
Printed by Edwards Bros., Ann Arbor, Mich.
Bound by Stanhope Bindery, Boston, Mass.